DATE DUE

JAN 0 9 REC'D			

THE GLENCOE LITERATURE LIBRARY

A Raisin in the Sun

with Related Readings

Glencoe
McGraw-Hill

New York, New York Columbus, Ohio Chicago, Illinois Peoria, Illinois Woodland Hills, California

Acknowledgments

Grateful acknowledgment is given authors, publishers, photographers, museums, and agents for permission to reprint the following copyrighted material. Every effort has been made to determine copyright owners. In case of any omissions, the Publisher will be pleased to make suitable acknowledgments in future editions.

Copyright © 1958, 1986 by Robert Nemiroff, as an unpublished work. Copyright © 1959, 1966, 1984, 1987, 1988 by Robert Nemiroff. Reprinted by arrangement of Random House Trade Publishing, a division of Random House, Inc. *Caution:* Professionals and amateurs are hereby warned that *A Raisin in the Sun*, being fully protected under the copyright Laws of the United States of America, the British Empire, including the Dominion of Canada, and all other countries of the Universal Copyright and Berne Conventions, is subject to royalty. All rights, including professional, amateur, motion picture, recitation, lecturing, public reading, radio and television broadcasting, and the rights of translation into foreign languages, are strictly reserved. Particular emphasis is laid on the question of readings, permission for which must be secured in writing. All inquiries should be addressed to the William Morris Agency, 1350 Avenue of the Americas, New York, NY 10019, authorized agents for the Estate of Lorraine Hansberry and for Robert Nemiroff, Executor.

"Commentary" by Spike Lee, copyright © 1992 by Spike Lee, from *A Raisin in the Sun: The Unfilmed Original Screenplay* by Lorraine Hansberry, introduced by Margaret B. Wilkerson, edited by Robert Nemiroff. Used by permission of Dutton Signet, a division of Penguin Putnam Inc.

Excerpted from *Lorraine Hansberry* by Susan Sinnott, copyright © 1999 by Susan Sinnott, by permission of Conari Press.

"Deferred" and "Note on Commercial Theatre" from *The Collected Poems of Langston Hughes* by Langston Hughes, copyright © 1994 by The Estate of Langston Hughes. Used by permission of Alfred A. Knopf, a division of Random House, Inc.

"Everyday Use" from *In Love & Trouble: Stories of Black Women*, copyright © 1973 by Alice Walker, reprinted by permission of Harcourt, Inc.

Excerpt from *Talking to High Monks in the Snow: An Asian American Odyssey* by Lydia Minatoya, copyright © 1992 by Lydia Minatoya. Reprinted by permission of HarperCollins Publishers, Inc.

Cover Art: *The Feast*, 1924, Anna Belle Lee Washington. SuperStock.

NOTE: *Lorraine Hansberry's pioneering drama is the story of an embattled African American family in the 1950s. Situations, language, and descriptions may be offensive to some readers.*

Glencoe/McGraw-Hill

A Division of The McGraw·Hill Companies

Send all inquiries to:
Glencoe/McGraw-Hill
8787 Orion Place
Columbus, OH 43240

ISBN 0-07-828404-X
Printed in the United States of America
11 12 13 14 026 12 11 10 09

Contents

A Raisin
in the Sun

Lorraine Hansberry

What happens to a dream deferred?
Does it dry up
Like a raisin in the sun?
Or fester like a sore—
And then run?
Does it stink like rotten meat
or crust and sugar over—
Like a syrupy sweet?

Maybe it just sags
Like a heavy load.

Or does it explode?

LANGSTON HUGHES

CAST

RUTH YOUNGER
TRAVIS YOUNGER
WALTER LEE YOUNGER (BROTHER)
BENEATHA YOUNGER
LENA YOUNGER (MAMA)
JOSEPH ASAGAI
GEORGE MURCHISON
KARL LINDNER
BOBO
MOVING MEN

The action of the play is set
in Chicago's Southside, sometime between
World War II and the present.

Act I
Scene One: Friday morning.
Scene Two: The following morning.

Act II
Scene One: Later, the same day.
Scene Two: Friday night, a few weeks later.
Scene Three: Moving day, one week later.

Act III
An hour later.

Act I

The YOUNGER *living room would be a comfortable and well-ordered room if it were not for a number of indestructible contradictions to this state of being. Its furnishings are typical and undistinguished and their primary feature now is that they have clearly had to accommodate the living of too many people for too many years—and they are tired. Still, we can see that at some time, a time probably no longer remembered by the family (except perhaps for* MAMA*), the furnishings of this room were actually selected with care and love and even hope—and brought to this apartment and arranged with taste and pride.*

That was a long time ago. Now the once loved pattern of the couch upholstery has to fight to show itself from under acres of crocheted doilies and couch covers which have themselves finally come to be more important than the upholstery. And here a table or a chair has been moved to disguise the worn places in the carpet; but the carpet has fought back by showing its weariness, with depressing uniformity, elsewhere on its surface.

Weariness has, in fact, won in this room. Everything has been polished, washed, sat on, used, scrubbed too often. All pretenses but living itself have long since vanished from the very atmosphere of this room.

Moreover, a section of this room, for it is not really a room unto itself, though the landlord's lease would make it seem so, slopes backward to provide a small kitchen area, where the family prepares the meals that are eaten in the living room proper, which must also serve as dining room. The single window that has been provided for these "two" rooms is located in this kitchen area. The sole natural light the family may enjoy in the course of a day is only that which fights its way through this little window.

At left, a door leads to a bedroom which is shared by MAMA *and her daughter,* BENEATHA. *At right, opposite, is a second room (which in the beginning of the life of this apartment was probably a breakfast room) which serves as a bedroom for* WALTER *and his wife,* RUTH.

Time: Sometime between World War II and the present.

Place: Chicago's Southside.

At Rise: It is morning dark in the living room. TRAVIS *is asleep on the make-down bed at center. An alarm clock sounds from within the bedroom at right, and presently* RUTH *enters from that room and closes the door behind her. She crosses sleepily toward the window. As she passes her sleeping son she reaches down and shakes him a little. At the window she raises the shade and a dusky Southside morning light comes in feebly. She fills a pot with water and puts it on to boil. She calls to the boy, between yawns, in a slightly muffled voice.*

RUTH *is about thirty. We can see that she was a pretty girl, even exceptionally so, but now it is apparent that life has been little that she expected, and disappointment has already begun to hang in her face. In a few years, before thirty-five even, she will be known among her people as a "settled woman."*

She crosses to her son and gives him a good, final, rousing shake.

RUTH Come on now, boy, it's seven thirty! (*Her son sits up at last, in a stupor of sleepiness*) I say hurry up, Travis! You ain't the only person in the world got to use a bathroom! (*The child, a sturdy, handsome little boy of ten or eleven, drags himself out of the bed and almost blindly takes his towels and "today's clothes" from drawers and a closet and goes out to the bathroom, which is in an outside hall and which is shared by another family or families on the same floor.* RUTH *crosses to the bedroom door at right and opens it and calls in to her husband*) Walter Lee! . . . It's after seven thirty! Lemme see you do some waking up in there now! (*She waits*) You better get up from there, man! It's after seven thirty I tell you. (*She waits again*) All right, you just go ahead and lay there and next thing you know Travis be finished and Mr. Johnson'll be in there and you'll be fussing and cussing round here like a madman! And be late too! (*She waits, at the end of patience*) Walter Lee—it's time for you to GET UP!

(*She waits another second and then starts to go into the bedroom, but is apparently satisfied that her husband has begun to get up. She stops, pulls the door to, and returns to the kitchen area. She wipes her face with a moist cloth and runs her fingers through her sleep-disheveled hair in a vain effort and ties an apron around her housecoat. The bedroom door at right opens and her husband stands in the doorway in his pajamas, which are rumpled and mismated. He is a lean, intense young man in his middle thirties, inclined to quick nervous movements and erratic speech habits—and always in his voice there is a quality of indictment*)

WALTER Is he out yet?

RUTH What do you mean *out?* He ain't hardly got in there good yet.

WALTER (*Wandering in, still more oriented to sleep than to a new day*) Well, what was you doing all that yelling for if I can't even get in there yet? (*Stopping and thinking*) Check coming today?

RUTH They *said* Saturday and this is just Friday and I hopes to God you ain't going to get up here first thing this morning and start talking to me 'bout no money—'cause I 'bout don't want to hear it.

WALTER Something the matter with you this morning?

RUTH No—I'm just sleepy as the devil. What kind of eggs you want?

WALTER Not scrambled. (RUTH *starts to scramble eggs*) Paper come? (RUTH *points impatiently to the rolled up* Tribune *on the table, and he gets it and spreads it out and vaguely reads the front page*) Set off another bomb yesterday.

RUTH (*Maximum indifference*) Did they?

WALTER (*Looking up*) What's the matter with you?

RUTH Ain't nothing the matter with me. And don't keep asking me that this morning.

WALTER Ain't nobody bothering you. (*Reading the news of the day absently again*) Say Colonel McCormick is sick.

RUTH (*Affecting tea-party interest*) Is he now? Poor thing.

WALTER (*Sighing and looking at his watch*) Oh, me. (*He waits*) Now what is that boy doing in that bathroom all this time? He just going to have to start getting up earlier. I can't be being late to work on account of him fooling around in there.

RUTH (*Turning on him*) Oh, no he ain't going to be getting up no earlier no such thing! It ain't his fault that he can't get to bed no earlier nights 'cause he got a bunch of crazy good-for-nothing clowns sitting up running their mouths in what is supposed to be his bedroom after ten o'clock at night . . .

WALTER That's what you mad about, ain't it? The things I want to talk about with my friends just couldn't be important in your mind, could they?

(*He rises and finds a cigarette in her handbag on the table and crosses to the little window and looks out, smoking and deeply enjoying the first one*)

RUTH (*Almost matter of factly, a complaint too automatic to deserve emphasis*) Why you always got to smoke before you eat in the morning?

WALTER (*At the window*) Just look at 'em down there . . . Running and racing to work . . . (*He turns and faces his wife and watches her a moment at the stove, and then, suddenly*) You look young this morning, baby.

RUTH (*Indifferently*) Yeah?

WALTER Just for a second—stirring them eggs. Just for a second it was—you looked real young again. (*He reaches for her; she crosses away. Then, drily*) It's gone now—you look like yourself again!

RUTH Man, if you don't shut up and leave me alone.

WALTER (*Looking out to the street again*) First thing a man ought to learn in life is not to make love to no colored woman first thing in the morning. You all some eeeevil people at eight o'clock in the morning.

(TRAVIS *appears in the hall doorway, almost fully dressed and quite wide awake now, his towels and pajamas across his shoulders. He opens the door and signals for his father to make the bathroom in a hurry*)

TRAVIS (*Watching the bathroom*) Daddy, come on!

(WALTER *gets his bathroom utensils and flies out to the bathroom*)

RUTH Sit down and have your breakfast, Travis.

TRAVIS Mama, this is Friday. (*Gleefully*) Check coming tomorrow, huh?

RUTH You get your mind off money and eat your breakfast.

TRAVIS (*Eating*) This is the morning we supposed to bring the fifty cents to school.

RUTH Well, I ain't got no fifty cents this morning.

TRAVIS Teacher say we have to.

RUTH I don't care what teacher say. I ain't got it. Eat your breakfast, Travis.

TRAVIS I *am* eating.

RUTH Hush up now and just eat!

(*The boy gives her an exasperated look for her lack of understanding, and eats grudgingly*)

TRAVIS You think Grandmama would have it?

RUTH No! And I want you to stop asking your grandmother for money, you hear me?

TRAVIS (*Outraged*) Gaaaleee! I don't ask her, she just gimme it sometimes!

RUTH Travis Willard Younger—I got too much on me this morning to be—

TRAVIS Maybe Daddy—

RUTH *Travis!*

(*The boy hushes abruptly. They are both quiet and tense for several seconds*)

TRAVIS (*Presently*) Could I maybe go carry some groceries in front of the supermarket for a little while after school then?

RUTH Just hush, I said. (*Travis jabs his spoon into his cereal bowl viciously, and rests his head in anger upon his fists*) If you through eating, you can get over there and make up your bed.

(*The boy obeys stiffly and crosses the room, almost mechanically, to the bed and more or less folds the bedding into a heap, then angrily gets his books and cap*)

TRAVIS (*Sulking and standing apart from her unnaturally*) I'm gone.

RUTH (*Looking up from the stove to inspect him automatically*) Come here. (*He crosses to her and she studies his head*) If you don't take this comb and fix this here head, you better! (*TRAVIS puts down his books with a great sigh of oppression, and crosses to the mirror. His mother mutters under her breath about his "slubbornness"*) 'Bout to march out of here with that head looking just like chickens slept in it! I just don't know where you get your slubborn ways . . . And get your jacket, too. Looks chilly out this morning.

TRAVIS (*With conspicuously brushed hair and jacket*) I'm gone.

RUTH Get carfare and milk money—(*Waving one finger*)—and not a single penny for no caps, you hear me?

TRAVIS (*With sullen politeness*) Yes'm.

(*He turns in outrage to leave. His mother watches after him as in his frustration he approaches the door almost comically. When she speaks to him, her voice has become a very gentle tease*)

RUTH (*Mocking; as she thinks he would say it*) Oh, Mama makes me so mad sometimes, I don't know what to do! (*She waits and continues to his back as he stands stock-still in front of the door*) I wouldn't kiss that woman good-bye for nothing in this world this morning! (*The boy finally turns around and rolls his eyes at her, knowing the mood has changed and he is vindicated; he does not, however, move toward her yet*) Not for nothing in this world! (*She finally laughs aloud at him and holds out her arms to him and we see that it is a way between them, very old and practiced. He crosses to her and allows her to embrace him warmly but keeps his face fixed with masculine* rigidity. *She holds him back from her presently and looks at him and runs her fingers over the features of his face. With utter gentleness—*) Now—whose little old angry man are you?

TRAVIS (*The masculinity and gruffness start to fade at last*) Aw gaalee— Mama . . .

RUTH (*Mimicking*) Aw gaaaaalleeeee, Mama! (*She pushes him, with rough playfulness and finality, toward the door*) Get on out of here or you going to be late.

TRAVIS (*In the face of love, new aggressiveness*) Mama, could I please go carry groceries?

RUTH Honey, it's starting to get so cold evenings.

WALTER (*Coming in from the bathroom and drawing a make-believe gun from a make-believe holster and shooting at his son*) What is it he wants to do?

RUTH Go carry groceries after school at the supermarket.

WALTER Well, let him go . . .

TRAVIS (*Quickly, to the ally*) I have to—she won't gimme the fifty cents . . .

WALTER (*To his wife only*) Why not?

RUTH (*Simply, and with flavor*) 'Cause we don't have it.

WALTER (*To* RUTH *only*) What you tell the boy things like that for? (*Reaching down into his pants with a rather important gesture*) Here, son—

(*He hands his boy the coin, but his eyes are directed to his wife's.* TRAVIS *takes the money happily*)

TRAVIS Thanks, Daddy.

(*He starts out.* RUTH *watches both of them with murder in her eyes.* WALTER *stands and stares back at her with defiance, and suddenly reaches into his pocket again on an afterthought*)

WALTER (*Without even looking at his son, still staring hard at his wife*) In fact, here's another fifty cents . . . Buy yourself some fruit today—or take a taxicab to school or something!

TRAVIS Whoopee—

(*He leaps up and clasps his father around the middle with his legs, and they face each other in mutual appreciation; slowly* WALTER LEE *peeks around the boy to catch the violent rays from his wife's eyes and draws his head back as if shot)*

WALTER You better get down now—and get to school, man.

TRAVIS *(At the door)* O.K. Good-bye.

(He exits)

WALTER *(After him, pointing with pride)* That's my boy. *(She looks at him in disgust and turns back to her work)* You know what I was thinking 'bout in the bathroom this morning?

RUTH No.

WALTER How come you always try to be so pleasant!

RUTH What is there to be pleasant 'bout!

WALTER You want to know what I was thinking 'bout in the bathroom or not!

RUTH I know what you thinking 'bout.

WALTER *(Ignoring her)* 'Bout what me and Willy Harris was talking about last night.

RUTH *(Immediately—a refrain)* Willy Harris is a good-for-nothing loud-mouth.

WALTER Anybody who talks to me has got to be a good-for-nothing loud-mouth, ain't he? And what you know about who is just a good-for-nothing loudmouth? Charlie Atkins was just a "good-for-nothing loudmouth" too, wasn't he! When he wanted me to go in the dry-cleaning business with him. And now—he's grossing a hundred thousand a year. A hundred thousand dollars a year! You still call *him* a loudmouth!

RUTH *(Bitterly)* Oh, Walter Lee . . .

(She folds her head on her arms over the table)

WALTER *(Rising and coming to her and standing over her)* You tired, ain't you? Tired of everything. Me, the boy, the way we live—this beat-up hole—everything. Ain't you? *(She doesn't look up, doesn't answer)* So tired—moaning and groaning all the time, but you wouldn't do nothing to help, would you? You couldn't be on my side that long for nothing, could you?

RUTH Walter, please leave me alone.

WALTER A man needs for a woman to back him up . . .

RUTH Walter—

WALTER Mama would listen to you. You know she listens to you more than she do me and Bennie. She think more of you. All you have to do is just sit down with her when you drinking your coffee one morning and talking 'bout things like you do and—(*He sits down beside her and demonstrates graphically what he thinks her methods and tone should be*)—you just sip your coffee, see, and say easy like that you been thinking 'bout that deal Walter Lee is so interested in, 'bout the store and all, and sip some more coffee, like what you saying ain't really that important to you— And the next thing you know, she be listening good and asking you questions and when I come home—I can tell her the details. This ain't no fly-by-night proposition, baby. I mean we figured it out, me and Willy and Bobo.

RUTH (*With a frown*) Bobo?

WALTER Yeah. You see, this little liquor store we got in mind cost seventy-five thousand and we figured the initial investment on the place to be 'bout thirty thousand, see. That be ten thousand each. Course, there's a couple of hundred you got to pay so's you don't spend your life just waiting for them clowns to let your license get approved—

RUTH You mean graft?

WALTER (*Frowning impatiently*) Don't call it that. See there, that just goes to show you what women understand about the world. Baby, don't *nothing* happen for you in this world 'less you pay *somebody* off!

RUTH Walter, leave me alone! (*She raises her head and stares at him vigorously—then says, more quietly*) *Eat* your eggs, they gonna be cold.

WALTER (*Straightening up from her and looking off*) That's it. There you are. Man say to his woman: I got me a dream. His woman say: Eat your eggs. (*Sadly, but gaining in power*) Man say: I got to take hold of this here world, baby! And a woman will say: Eat your eggs and go to work. (*Passionately now*) Man say: I got to change my life, I'm choking to death, baby. And his woman say—(*In utter anguish as he brings his fists down on his thighs*)—Your eggs is getting cold!

RUTH (*Softly*) Walter, that ain't none of our money.

WALTER (*Not listening at all or even looking at her*) This morning, I was lookin' in the mirror and thinking about it . . . I'm thirty-five years old; I been married eleven years and I got a boy who sleeps in the living room—(*Very, very quietly*)—and all I got to give him is stories about how rich white people live . . .

RUTH Eat your eggs, Walter.

WALTER (*Slams the table and jumps up*)—DAMN MY EGGS—DAMN ALL THE EGGS THAT EVER WAS!

RUTH Then go to work.

WALTER (*Looking up at her*) See—I'm trying to talk to you 'bout myself—(*Shaking his head with the repetition*)—and all you can say is eat them eggs and go to work.

RUTH (*Wearily*) Honey, you never say nothing new. I listen to you every day, every night and every morning, and you never say nothing new. (*Shrugging*) So you would rather be Mr. Arnold than be his chauffeur. So—I would *rather* be living in Buckingham Palace.

WALTER That is just what is wrong with the colored woman in this world . . . Don't understand about building their men up and making 'em feel like they somebody. Like they can do something.

RUTH (*Drily, but to hurt*) There *are* colored men who do things.

WALTER No thanks to the colored woman.

RUTH Well, being a colored woman, I guess I can't help myself none.

(*She rises and gets the ironing board and sets it up and attacks a huge pile of rough-dried clothes, sprinkling them in preparation for the ironing and then rolling them into tight fat balls*)

WALTER (*Mumbling*) We one group of men tied to a race of women with small minds!

(*His sister* BENEATHA *enters. She is about twenty, as slim and intense as her brother. She is not as pretty as her sister-in-law, but her lean, almost intellectual face has a handsomeness of its own. She wears a bright-red flannel nightie, and her thick hair stands wildly about her head. Her speech is a mixture of many things; it is different from the rest of the family's insofar as education has permeated her sense of English—and perhaps the Midwest rather than the South has finally—at last—won out in her inflection; but not altogether, because over all of it is a soft slurring and transformed use of vowels which is the decided influence of the Southside. She passes through the room without looking at either* RUTH *or* WALTER *and goes to the outside door and looks, a little blindly, out to the bathroom. She sees that it has been lost to the Johnsons. She closes the door with a sleepy vengeance and crosses to the table and sits down a little defeated)*

BENEATHA I am going to start timing those people.

WALTER You should get up earlier.

BENEATHA *(Her face in her hands. She is still fighting the urge to go back to bed)* Really—would you suggest dawn? Where's the paper?

WALTER *(Pushing the paper across the table to her as he studies her almost clinically, as though he has never seen her before)* You a horrible-looking chick at this hour.

BENEATHA *(Drily)* Good morning, everybody.

WALTER *(Senselessly)* How is school coming?

BENEATHA *(In the same spirit)* Lovely. Lovely. And you know, biology is the greatest. *(Looking up at him)* I dissected something that looked just like you yesterday.

WALTER I just wondered if you've made up your mind and everything.

BENEATHA *(Gaining in sharpness and impatience)* And what did I answer yesterday morning—and the day before that?

RUTH *(From the ironing board, like someone disinterested and old)* Don't be so nasty, Bennie.

BENEATHA *(Still to her brother)* And the day before that and the day before that!

WALTER *(Defensively)* I'm interested in you. Something wrong with that? Ain't many girls who decide—

WALTER *and* **BENEATHA** *(In unison)*—"to be a doctor." *(Silence)*

WALTER Have we figured out yet just exactly how much medical school is going to cost?

RUTH Walter Lee, why don't you leave that girl alone and get out of here to work?

BENEATHA *(Exits to the bathroom and bangs on the door)* Come on out of there, please!

(She comes back into the room)

WALTER *(Looking at his sister intently)* You know the check is coming tomorrow.

BENEATHA (*Turning on him with a sharpness all her own*) That money belongs to Mama, Walter, and it's for her to decide how she wants to use it. I don't care if she wants to buy a house or a rocket ship or just nail it up somewhere and look at it. It's hers. Not ours—*hers*.

WALTER (*Bitterly*) Now ain't that fine! You just got your mother's interest at heart, ain't you, girl? You such a nice girl—but if Mama got that money she can always take a few thousand and help you through school too—can't she?

BENEATHA I have never asked anyone around here to do anything for me!

WALTER No! And the line between asking and just accepting when the time comes is big and wide—ain't it!

BENEATHA (*With fury*) What do you want from me, Brother—that I quit school or just drop dead, which!

WALTER I don't want nothing but for you to stop acting holy 'round here. Me and Ruth done made some sacrifices for you—why can't you do something for the family?

RUTH Walter, don't be dragging me in it.

WALTER You are in it—Don't you get up and go to work in somebody's kitchen for the last three years to help put clothes on her back?

RUTH Oh, Walter—that's not fair . . .

WALTER It ain't that nobody expects you to get on your knees and say thank you, Brother; thank you, Ruth; thank you, Mama—and thank you, Travis, for wearing the same pair of shoes for two semesters—

BENEATHA (*Dropping to her knees*) Well—I *do*—all right?—thank everybody! And forgive me for ever wanting to be anything at all! (*Pursuing him on her knees across the floor*) FORGIVE ME, FORGIVE ME, FORGIVE ME!

RUTH Please stop it! Your mama'll hear you.

WALTER Who the hell told you you had to be a doctor? If you so crazy 'bout messing 'round with sick people—then go be a nurse like other women—or just get married and be quiet . . .

BENEATHA Well—you finally got it said . . . It took you three years but you finally got it said. Walter, give up; leave me alone—it's Mama's money.

WALTER *He was my father, too!*

BENEATHA So what? He was mine, too—and Travis' grandfather—but the insurance money belongs to Mama. Picking on me is not going to make her give it to you to invest in any liquor stores—(*Underbreath, dropping into a chair*)—and I for one say, God bless Mama for that!

WALTER (*To* RUTH) See—did you hear? Did you hear!

RUTH Honey, please go to work.

WALTER Nobody in this house is ever going to understand me.

BENEATHA Because you're a nut.

WALTER Who's a nut?

BENEATHA You—you are a nut. Thee is mad, boy.

WALTER (*Looking at his wife and his sister from the door, very sadly*) The world's most backward race of people, and that's a fact.

BENEATHA (*Turning slowly in her chair*) And then there are all those prophets who would lead us out of the wilderness—(WALTER *slams out of the house*)—into the swamps!

RUTH Bennie, why you always gotta be pickin' on your brother? Can't you be a little sweeter sometimes? (*Door opens.* WALTER *walks in. He fumbles with his cap, starts to speak, clears throat, looks everywhere but at* RUTH. *Finally:*)

WALTER (*To Ruth*) I need some money for carfare.

RUTH (*Looks at him, then warms, teasing, but tenderly*) Fifty cents? (*She goes to her bag and gets money*) Here—take a taxi!

(WALTER *exits.* MAMA *enters. She is a woman in her early sixties, full-bodied and strong. She is one of those women of a certain grace and beauty who wear it so unobtrusively that it takes a while to notice. Her dark-brown face is surrounded by the total whiteness of her hair, and, being a woman who has adjusted to many things in life and overcome many more, her face is full of strength. She has, we can see, wit and faith of a kind that keep her eyes lit and full of interest and expectancy. She is, in a word, a beautiful woman. Her bearing is perhaps most like the noble bearing of the women of the Hereros of Southwest Africa—rather as if she imagines that as she walks she still bears a basket or a vessel upon her head. Her speech, on the other hand, is as careless as her carriage is precise—she is inclined to slur everything—but her voice is perhaps not so much quiet as simply soft*)

MAMA Who that 'round here slamming doors at this hour?

(She crosses through the room, goes to the window, opens it, and brings in a feeble little plant growing doggedly in a small pot on the windowsill. She feels the dirt and puts it back out)

RUTH   That was Walter Lee. He and Bennie was at it again.

MAMA   My children and they tempers. Lord, if this little old plant don't get more sun than it's been getting it ain't never going to see spring again. *(She turns from the window)* What's the matter with you this morning, Ruth? You looks right peaked. You aiming to iron all them things? Leave some for me. I'll get to 'em this afternoon. Bennie honey, it's too drafty for you to be sitting 'round half dressed. Where's your robe?

BENEATHA   In the cleaners.

MAMA   Well, go get mine and put it on.

BENEATHA   I'm not cold, Mama, honest.

MAMA   I know—but you so thin . . .

BENEATHA   *(Irritably)* Mama, I'm not cold.

MAMA   *(Seeing the make-down bed as* TRAVIS *has left it)* Lord have mercy, look at that poor bed. Bless his heart—he tries, don't he?

(She moves to the bed TRAVIS *has sloppily made up)*

RUTH   No—he don't half try at all 'cause he knows you going to come along behind him and fix everything. That's just how come he don't know how to do nothing right now—you done spoiled that boy so.

MAMA   *(Folding bedding)* Well—he's a little boy. Ain't supposed to know 'bout housekeeping. My baby, that's what he is. What you fix for his breakfast this morning?

RUTH   *(Angrily)* I feed my son, Lena!

MAMA   I ain't meddling—*(Underbreath; busy-bodyish)* I just noticed all last week he had cold cereal, and when it starts getting this chilly in the fall a child ought to have some hot grits or something when he goes out in the cold—

RUTH   *(Furious)* I gave him hot oats—is that all right!

MAMA   I ain't meddling. *(Pause)* Put a lot of nice butter on it? (RUTH *shoots her an angry look and does not reply)* He likes lots of butter.

RUTH   *(Exasperated)* Lena—

MAMA (*To* BENEATHA. MAMA *is inclined to wander conversationally some-times*) What was you and your brother fussing 'bout this morning?

BENEATHA It's not important, Mama.

(*She gets up and goes to look out at the bathroom, which is apparently free, and she picks up her towels and rushes out*)

MAMA What was they fighting about?

RUTH Now you know as well as I do.

MAMA (*Shaking her head*) Brother still worrying hisself sick about that money?

RUTH You know he is.

MAMA You had breakfast?

RUTH Some coffee.

MAMA Girl, you better start eating and looking after yourself better. You almost as thin as Travis.

RUTH Lena—

MAMA Un-hunh?

RUTH What are you going to do with it?

MAMA Now don't you start, child. It's too early in the morning to be talk-ing about money. It ain't Christian.

RUTH It's just that he got his heart set on that store—

MAMA You mean that liquor store that Willy Harris want him to invest in?

RUTH Yes—

MAMA We ain't no business people, Ruth. We just plain working folks.

RUTH Ain't nobody business people till they go into business. Walter Lee say colored people ain't never going to start getting ahead till they start gambling on some different kinds of things in the world—investments and things.

MAMA What done got into you girl? Walter Lee done finally sold you on investing.

RUTH No. Mama, something is happening between Walter and me. I don't know what it is—but he needs something—something I can't give him anymore. He needs this chance, Lena.

MAMA *(Frowning deeply)* But liquor, honey—

RUTH Well—like Walter say—I spec people going to always be drinking themselves some liquor.

MAMA Well—whether they drinks it or not ain't none of my business. But whether I go into business selling it to 'em *is,* and I don't want that on my ledger this late in life. *(Stopping suddenly and studying her daughter-in-law)* Ruth Younger, what's the matter with you today? You look like you could fall over right there.

RUTH I'm tired.

MAMA Then you better stay home from work today.

RUTH I can't stay home. She'd be calling up the agency and screaming at them, "My girl didn't come in today—send me somebody! My girl didn't come in!" Oh, she just have a fit . . .

MAMA Well, let her have it. I'll just call her up and say you got the flu—

RUTH *(Laughing)* Why the flu?

MAMA 'Cause it sounds respectable to 'em. Something white people get, too. They know 'bout the flu. Otherwise they think you been cut up or something when you tell 'em you sick.

RUTH I got to go in. We need the money.

MAMA Somebody would of thought my children done all but starved to death the way they talk about money here late. Child, we got a great big old check coming tomorrow.

RUTH *(Sincerely, but also self-righteously)* Now that's your money. It ain't got nothing to do with me. We all feel like that—Walter and Bennie and me—even Travis.

MAMA *(Thoughtfully, and suddenly very far away)* Ten thousand dollars—

RUTH Sure is wonderful.

MAMA Ten thousand dollars.

RUTH You know what you should do, Miss Lena? You should take yourself a trip somewhere. To Europe or South America or someplace—

MAMA *(Throwing up her hands at the thought)* Oh, child!

RUTH I'm serious. Just pack up and leave! Go on away and enjoy yourself some. Forget about the family and have yourself a ball for once in your life—

MAMA (*Drily*) You sound like I'm just about ready to die. Who'd go with me? What I look like wandering 'round Europe by myself?

RUTH Shoot—these here rich white women do it all the time. They don't think nothing of packing up they suitcases and piling on one of them big steamships and—swoosh!—they gone, child.

MAMA Something always told me I wasn't no rich white woman.

RUTH Well—what are you going to do with it then?

MAMA I ain't rightly decided. (*Thinking. She speaks now with emphasis*) Some of it got to be put away for Beneatha and her schoolin'—and ain't nothing going to touch that part of it. Nothing. (*She waits several seconds, trying to make up her mind about something, and looks at* RUTH *a little tentatively before going on*) Been thinking that we maybe could meet the notes on a little old two-story somewhere, with a yard where Travis could play in the summertime, if we use part of the insurance for a down payment and everybody kind of pitch in. I could maybe take on a little day work again, few days a week—

RUTH (*Studying her mother-in-law furtively and concentrating on her ironing, anxious to encourage without seeming to*) Well, Lord knows, we've put enough rent into this here rat trap to pay for four houses by now . . .

MAMA (*Looking up at the words "rat trap" and then looking around and leaning back and sighing—in a suddenly reflective mood—*) "Rat trap"—yes, that's all it is. (*Smiling*) I remember just as well the day me and Big Walter moved in here. Hadn't been married but two weeks and wasn't planning on living here no more than a year. (*She shakes her head at the dissolved dream*) We was going to set away, little by little, don't you know, and buy a little place out in Morgan Park. We had even picked out the house. (*Chuckling a little*) Looks right dumpy today. But Lord, child, you should know all the dreams I had 'bout buying that house and fixing it up and making me a little garden in the back—(*She waits and stops smiling*) And didn't none of it happen.

(*Dropping her hands in a futile gesture*)

RUTH (*Keeps her head down, ironing*) Yes, life can be a barrel of disappointments, sometimes.

MAMA Honey, Big Walter would come in here some nights back then and slump down on that couch there and just look at the rug, and look at me and look at the rug and then back at me—and I'd know he was down then . . . really down. (*After a second very long and thoughtful pause; she is seeing back to times that only she can see*) And then, Lord, when I lost that baby—little Claude—I almost thought I was going to lose Big Walter too. Oh, that man grieved hisself! He was one man to love his children.

RUTH Ain't nothin' can tear at you like losin' your baby.

MAMA I guess that's how come that man finally worked hisself to death like he done. Like he was fighting his own war with this here world that took his baby from him.

RUTH He sure was a fine man, all right. I always liked Mr. Younger.

MAMA Crazy 'bout his children! God knows there was plenty wrong with Walter Younger—hard-headed, mean, kind of wild with women— plenty wrong with him. But he sure loved his children. Always wanted them to have something—be something. That's where Brother gets all those notions, I reckon. Big Walter used to say, he'd get right wet in the eyes sometimes, lean his head back with the water standing in his eyes and say, "Seem like God didn't see fit to give the black man nothing but dreams—but He did give us children to make them dreams seem worth while." (*She smiles*) He could talk like that, don't you know.

RUTH Yes, he sure could. He was a good man, Mr. Younger.

MAMA Yes, a fine man—just couldn't never catch up with his dreams, that's all.

(BENEATHA *comes in, brushing her hair and looking up to the ceiling, where the sound of a vacuum cleaner has started up*)

BENEATHA What could be so dirty on that woman's rugs that she has to vacuum them every single day?

RUTH I wish certain young women 'round here who I could name would take inspiration about certain rugs in a certain apartment I could also mention.

BENEATHA (*Shrugging*) How much cleaning can a house need, for Christ's sakes.

MAMA (*Not liking the Lord's name used thus*) Bennie!

RUTH Just listen to her—just listen!

BENEATHA Oh, God!

MAMA If you use the Lord's name just one more time—

BENEATHA (*A bit of a whine*) Oh, Mama—

RUTH Fresh—just fresh as salt, this girl!

BENEATHA (*Drily*) Well—if the salt loses its savor—

MAMA Now that will do. I just ain't going to have you 'round here reciting the scriptures in vain—you hear me?

BENEATHA How did I manage to get on everybody's wrong side by just walking into a room?

RUTH If you weren't so fresh—

BENEATHA Ruth, I'm twenty years old.

MAMA What time you be home from school today?

BENEATHA Kind of late. (*With enthusiasm*) Madeline is going to start my guitar lessons today.

(*MAMA and RUTH look up with the same expression*)

MAMA Your *what* kind of lessons?

BENEATHA Guitar.

RUTH Oh, Father!

MAMA How come you done taken it in your mind to learn to play the guitar?

BENEATHA I just want to, that's all.

MAMA (*Smiling*) Lord, child, don't you know what to do with yourself? How long it going to be before you get tired of this now—like you got tired of that little play-acting group you joined last year? (*Looking at RUTH*) And what was it the year before that?

RUTH The horseback-riding club for which she bought that fifty-five dollar riding habit that's been hanging in the closet ever since!

MAMA (*To BENEATHA*) Why you got to flit so from one thing to another, baby?

BENEATHA (*Sharply*) I just want to learn to play the guitar. Is there anything wrong with that?

MAMA Ain't nobody trying to stop you. I just wonders sometimes why you has to flit so from one thing to another all the time. You ain't never done nothing with that camera equipment you brought home—

BENEATHA I don't flit! I—I experiment with different forms of expression—

RUTH Like riding a horse?

BENEATHA —People have to express themselves one way or another.

MAMA What is it you want to express?

BENEATHA (*Angrily*) Me! (MAMA *and* RUTH *look at each other and burst into raucous laughter*) Don't worry—I don't expect you to understand.

MAMA (*To change the subject*) Who you going out with tomorrow night?

BENEATHA (*With displeasure*) George Murchison again.

MAMA (*Pleased*) Oh—you getting a little sweet on him?

RUTH You ask me, this child ain't sweet on nobody but herself— (*Underbreath*) Express herself!

(*They laugh*)

BENEATHA Oh—I like George all right, Mama. I mean I like him enough to go out with him and stuff, but—

RUTH (*For devilment*) What does *and stuff* mean?

BENEATHA Mind your own business.

MAMA Stop picking at her now, Ruth. (*She chuckles—then a suspicious sudden look at her daughter as she turns in her chair for emphasis*) What DOES it mean?

BENEATHA (*Wearily*) Oh, I just mean I couldn't ever really be serious about George. He's—he's so shallow.

RUTH Shallow—what do you mean he's shallow? He's *rich!*

MAMA Hush, Ruth.

BENEATHA I know he's rich. He knows he's rich, too.

RUTH Well—what other qualities a man got to have to satisfy you, little girl?

BENEATHA You wouldn't even begin to understand. Anybody who married Walter could not possibly understand.

MAMA   (*Outraged*) What kind of way is that to talk about your brother?

BENEATHA   Brother is a flip—let's face it.

MAMA   (*To* RUTH, *helplessly*) What's a flip?

RUTH   (*Glad to add kindling*) She's saying he's crazy.

BENEATHA   Not crazy. Brother isn't really crazy yet—he—he's an elaborate neurotic.

MAMA   Hush your mouth!

BENEATHA   As for George. Well. George looks good—he's got a beautiful car and he takes me to nice places and, as my sister-in-law says, he is probably the richest boy I will ever get to know and I even like him sometimes—but if the Youngers are sitting around waiting to see if their little Bennie is going to tie up the family with the Murchisons, they are wasting their time.

RUTH   You mean you wouldn't marry George Murchison if he asked you someday? That pretty, rich thing? Honey, I knew you was odd—

BENEATHA   No I would not marry him if all I felt for him was what I feel now. Besides, George's family wouldn't really like it.

MAMA   Why not?

BENEATHA   Oh, Mama—The Murchison's are honest-to-God-real-*live*-rich colored people, and the only people in the world who are more snobbish than rich white people are rich colored people. I thought everybody knew that. I've met Mrs. Murchison. She's a scene!

MAMA   You must not dislike people 'cause they well off, honey.

BENEATHA   Why not? It makes just as much sense as disliking people 'cause they are poor, and lots of people do that.

RUTH   (*A wisdom-of-the-ages manner. To* MAMA) Well, she'll get over some of this—

BENEATHA   Get over it? What are you talking about, Ruth? Listen, I'm going to be a doctor. I'm not worried about who I'm going to marry yet—if I ever get married.

MAMA *and* RUTH   If!

MAMA   Now, Bennie—

BENEATHA Oh, I probably will . . . but first I'm going to be a doctor, and George, for one, still thinks that's pretty funny. I couldn't be bothered with that. I am going to be a doctor and everybody around here better understand that!

MAMA (*Kindly*) 'Course you going to be a doctor, honey, God willing.

BENEATHA (*Drily*) God hasn't got a thing to do with it.

MAMA Beneatha—that just wasn't necessary.

BENEATHA Well—neither is God. I get sick of hearing about God.

MAMA Beneatha!

BENEATHA I mean it! I'm just tired of hearing about God all the time. What has He got to do with anything? Does he pay tuition?

MAMA You 'bout to get your fresh little jaw slapped!

RUTH That's just what she needs, all right!

BENEATHA Why? Why can't I say what I want to around here, like everybody else?

MAMA It don't sound nice for a young girl to say things like that—you wasn't brought up that way. Me and your father went to trouble to get you and Brother to church every Sunday.

BENEATHA Mama, you don't understand. It's all a matter of ideas, and God is just one idea I don't accept. It's not important. I am not going out and be immoral or commit crimes because I don't believe in God. I don't even think about it. It's just that I get tired of Him getting credit for all the things the human race achieves through its own stubborn effort. There simply is no blasted God—there is only man and it is *he* who makes miracles!

(MAMA *absorbs this speech, studies her daughter and rises slowly and crosses to* BENEATHA *and slaps her powerfully across the face. After, there is only silence and the daughter drops her eyes from her mother's face, and* MAMA *is very tall before her*)

MAMA Now—you say after me, in my mother's house there is still God. (*There is a long pause and* BENEATHA *stares at the floor wordlessly.* MAMA *repeats the phrase with precision and cool emotion*) In my mother's house there is still God.

BENEATHA In my mother's house there is still God.

(*A long pause*)

MAMA (*Walking away from* BENEATHA, *too disturbed for triumphant posture. Stopping and turning back to her daughter*) There are some ideas we ain't going to have in this house. Not long as I am at the head of this family.

BENEATHA Yes, ma'am.

(MAMA *walks out of the room*)

RUTH (*Almost gently, with profound understanding*) You think you a woman, Bennie—but you still a little girl. What you did was childish—so you got treated like a child.

BENEATHA I see. (*Quietly*) I also see that everybody thinks it's all right for Mama to be a tyrant. But all the tyranny in the world will never put a God in the heavens!

(*She picks up her books and goes out. Pause*)

RUTH (*Goes to* MAMA's *door*) She said she was sorry.

MAMA (*Coming out, going to her plant*) They frightens me, Ruth. My children.

RUTH You got good children, Lena. They just a little off sometimes—but they're good.

MAMA No—there's something come down between me and them that don't let us understand each other and I don't know what it is. One done almost lost his mind thinking 'bout money all the time and the other done commence to talk about things I can't seem to understand in no form or fashion. What is it that's changing, Ruth.

RUTH (*Soothingly, older than her years*) Now . . . you taking it all too seriously. You just got strong-willed children and it takes a strong woman like you to keep 'em in hand.

MAMA (*Looking at her plant and sprinkling a little water on it*) They spirited all right, my children. Got to admit they got spirit—Bennie and Walter. Like this little old plant that ain't never had enough sunshine or nothing—and look at it . . .

(*She has her back to* RUTH, *who has had to stop ironing and lean against something and put the back of her hand to her forehead*)

RUTH (*Trying to keep* MAMA *from noticing*) You . . . sure . . . loves that little old thing, don't you? . . .

MAMA Well, I always wanted me a garden like I used to see sometimes at the back of the houses down home. This plant is close as I ever got to having one. (*She looks out of the window as she replaces the plant*) Lord, ain't nothing as dreary as the view from this window on a dreary day, is there? Why ain't you singing this morning, Ruth? Sing that "No Ways Tired." That song always lifts me up so—(*She turns at last to see that* RUTH *has slipped quietly to the floor, in a state of semiconsciousness*) Ruth! Ruth honey—what's the matter with you . . . Ruth!

Curtain

SCENE TWO

It is the following morning; a Saturday morning, and house cleaning is in progress at the YOUNGERS. *Furniture has been shoved hither and yon and* MAMA *is giving the kitchen-area walls a washing down.* BENEATHA, *in dungarees, with a hand-kerchief tied around her face, is spraying insecticide into the cracks in the walls. As they work, the radio is on and a Southside disk-jockey program is inappropriately filling the house with a rather exotic saxophone blues.* TRAVIS, *the sole idle one, is leaning on his arms, looking out of the window.*

TRAVIS Grandmama, that stuff Bennie's using smells awful. Can I go down-stairs, please?

MAMA Did you get all them chores done already? I ain't seen you doing much.

TRAVIS Yes'm—finished early. Where did Mama go this morning?

MAMA (*Looking at* BENEATHA) She had to go on a little errand.

(*The phone rings.* BENEATHA *runs to answer it and reaches it before* WALTER, *who has entered from bedroom*)

TRAVIS Where?

MAMA To tend to her business.

BENEATHA Haylo . . . (*Disappointed*) Yes, he is. (*She tosses the phone to* WALTER, *who barely catches it*) It's Willie Harris again.

WALTER (*As privately as possible under* MAMA'S *gaze*) Hello, Willie. Did you get the papers from the lawyer? . . . No, not yet. I told you the mailman doesn't get here till ten-thirty . . . No, I'll come there . . . Yeah! Right away. (*He hangs up and goes for his coat*)

BENEATHA Brother, where did Ruth go?

WALTER (*As he exits*) How should I know!

TRAVIS Aw come on, Grandma. Can I go outside?

MAMA Oh, I guess so. You stay right in front of the house, though, and keep a good lookout for the postman.

TRAVIS Yes'm. (*He darts into bedroom for stickball and bat, reenters, and sees* BENEATHA *on her knees spraying under sofa with behind upraised. He edges closer to the target, takes aim, and lets her have it. She screams*) Leave them poor little cockroaches alone, they ain't bothering you none! (*He runs as she swings the spray gun at him viciously and playfully*) Grandma! Grandma!

MAMA   Look out there, girl, before you be spilling some of that stuff on that child!

TRAVIS   (*Safely behind the bastion of* MAMA) That's right—look out, now! (*He exits*)

BENEATHA   (*Drily*) I can't imagine that it would hurt him—it has never hurt the roaches.

MAMA   Well, little boys' hides ain't as tough as Southside roaches. You better get over there behind the bureau. I seen one marching out of there like Napoleon yesterday.

BENEATHA   There's really only one way to get rid of them, Mama—

MAMA   How?

BENEATHA   Set fire to this building! Mama, where did Ruth go?

MAMA   (*Looking at her with meaning*) To the doctor, I think.

BENEATHA   The doctor? What's the matter? (*They exchange glances*) You don't think—

MAMA   (*With her sense of drama*) Now I ain't saying what I think. But I ain't never been wrong 'bout a woman neither.

(*The phone rings*)

BENEATHA   (*At the phone*) Hay-lo . . . (*Pause, and a moment of recognition*) Well—when did you get back! . . . And how was it? . . . Of course I've missed you—in my way . . . This morning? No . . . house cleaning and all that and Mama hates it if I let people come over when the house is like this . . . You *have*? Well, that's different . . . What is it—Oh, what the hell, come on over . . . Right, see you then. *Arrivederci.*

(*She hangs up*)

MAMA   (*Who has listened vigorously, as is her habit*) Who is that you inviting over here with this house looking like this? You ain't got the pride you was born with!

BENEATHA   Asagai doesn't care how houses look, Mama—he's an intellectual.

MAMA   Who?

BENEATHA   Asagai—Joseph Asagai. He's an African boy I met on campus. He's been studying in Canada all summer.

MAMA   What's his name?

BENEATHA   Asagai, Joseph. Ah-sah-guy . . . He's from Nigeria.

MAMA   Oh, that's the little country that was founded by slaves way back . . .

BENEATHA   No, Mama—that's Liberia.

MAMA   I don't think I never met no African before.

BENEATHA   Well, do me a favor and don't ask him a whole lot of ignorant questions about Africans. I mean, do they wear clothes and all that—

MAMA   Well, now, I guess if you think we so ignorant 'round here maybe you shouldn't bring your friends here—

BENEATHA   It's just that people ask such crazy things. All anyone seems to know about when it comes to Africa is Tarzan—

MAMA   (*Indignantly*) Why should I know anything about Africa?

BENEATHA   Why do you give money at church for the missionary work?

MAMA   Well, that's to help save people.

BENEATHA   You mean save them from *heathenism*—

MAMA   (*Innocently*) Yes.

BENEATHA   I'm afraid they need more salvation from the British and the French.

(RUTH *comes in forlornly and pulls off her coat with dejection. They both turn to look at her*)

RUTH   (*Dispiritedly*) Well, I guess from all the happy faces—everybody knows.

BENEATHA   You're pregnant?

MAMA   Lord have mercy, I sure hope it's a little old girl. Travis ought to have a sister.

(BENEATHA *and* RUTH *give her a hopeless look for this grandmotherly enthusiasm*)

BENEATHA   How far along are you?

RUTH   Two months.

BENEATHA   Did you mean to? I mean did you plan it or was it an accident?

MAMA   What do you know about planning or not planning?

BENEATHA Oh, Mama.

RUTH (*Wearily*) She's twenty years old, Lena.

BENEATHA Did you plan it, Ruth?

RUTH Mind your own business.

BENEATHA It is my business—where is he going to live, on the *roof*? (*There is silence following the remark as the three women react to the sense of it*) Gee—I didn't mean that, Ruth, honest. Gee, I don't feel like that at all. I—I think it is wonderful.

RUTH (*Dully*) Wonderful.

BENEATHA Yes—really. (*There is a sudden commotion from the street and she goes to the window to look out*) What on earth is going on out there? These kids. (*There are, as she throws open the window, the shouts of children rising up from the street. She sticks her head out to see better and calls out*) TRAVIS! TRAVIS . . . WHAT ARE YOU DOING DOWN THERE? (*She sees*) Oh Lord, they're chasing a rat!

(RUTH *covers her face with hands and turns away*)

MAMA (*Angrily*) Tell that youngun to get himself up here, at once!

BENEATHA TRAVIS . . . YOU COME UPSTAIRS . . . AT ONCE!

RUTH (*Her face twisted*) Chasing a rat . . .

MAMA (*Looking at* RUTH, *worried*) Doctor say everything going to be all right?

RUTH (*Far away*) Yes—she says everything is going to be fine . . .

MAMA (*Immediately suspicious*) "She"—What doctor you went to?

(RUTH *just looks at* MAMA *meaningfully and* MAMA *opens her mouth to speak as* TRAVIS *bursts in*)

TRAVIS (*Excited and full of narrative, coming directly to his mother*) Mama, you should of seen the rat . . . Big as a cat, honest! (*He shows an exaggerated size with his hands*) Gaaleee, that rat was really cuttin' and Bubber caught him with his heel and the janitor, Mr. Barnett, got him with a stick—and then they got him in a corner and—BAM! BAM! BAM!—and he was still jumping around and bleeding like everything too—there's rat blood all over the street—

(RUTH *reaches out suddenly and grabs her son without even looking at him and clamps her hand over his mouth and holds him to her.* MAMA *crosses to them rapidly and takes the boy from her*)

MAMA You hush up now . . . talking all that terrible stuff . . . (TRAVIS *is staring at his mother with a stunned expression.* BENEATHA *comes quickly and takes him away from his grandmother and ushers him to the door*)

BENEATHA You go back outside and play . . . but not with any rats. (*She pushes him gently out the door with the boy straining to see what is wrong with his mother*)

MAMA (*Worriedly hovering over* RUTH) Ruth honey—what's the matter with you—you sick?

(RUTH *has her fists clenched on her thighs and fighting hard to suppress a scream that seems to be rising in her*)

BENEATHA What's the matter with her, Mama?

MAMA (*Working her fingers in* RUTH's *shoulders to relax her*) She be all right. Women gets right depressed sometimes when they get her way. (*Speaking softly, expertly, rapidly*) Now you just relax. That's right . . . just lean back, don't think 'bout nothing at all . . . nothing at all—

RUTH I'm all right . . .

(*The glassy-eyed look melts and then she collapses into a fit of heavy sobbing. The bell rings*)

BENEATHA Oh, my God—that must be Asagai.

MAMA (*To* RUTH) Come on now, honey. You need to lie down and rest awhile . . . then have some nice hot food.

(*They exit,* RUTH'S *weight on her mother-in-law.* BENEATHA, *herself profoundly disturbed, opens the door to admit a rather dramatic-looking young man with a large package*)

ASAGAI Hello, Alaiyo—

BENEATHA (*Holding the door open and regarding him with pleasure*) Hello . . . (*Long pause*) Well—come in. And please excuse everything. My mother was very upset about my letting anyone come here with the place like this.

ASAGAI (*Coming into the room*) You look disturbed too . . . Is something wrong?

BENEATHA (*Still at the door, absently*) Yes . . . we've all got acute ghetto-itis. (*She smiles and comes toward him, finding a cigarette and sitting*) So—sit down! No! Wait! (*She whips the spray gun off sofa where she had left it and puts the cushions back. At last perches on arm of sofa. He sits*) So, how was Canada?

ASAGAI (*A sophisticate*) Canadian.

BENEATHA (*Looking at him*) Asagai, I'm very glad you are back.

ASAGAI (*Looking back at her in turn*) Are you really?

BENEATHA Yes—very.

ASAGAI Why?—you were quite glad when I went away. What happened?

BENEATHA You went away.

ASAGAI Ahhhhhhhh.

BENEATHA Before—you wanted to be so serious before there was time.

ASAGAI How much time must there be before one knows what one feels?

BENEATHA (*Stalling this particular conversation. Her hands pressed together, in a deliberately childish gesture*) What did you bring me?

ASAGAI (*Handing her the package*) Open it and see.

BENEATHA (*Eagerly opening the package and drawing out some records and the colorful robes of a Nigerian woman*) Oh, Asagai! . . . You got them for me! . . . How beautiful . . . and the records too! (*She lifts out the robes and runs to the mirror with them and holds the drapery up in front of herself*)

ASAGAI (*Coming to her at the mirror*) I shall have to teach you how to drape it properly. (*He flings the material about her for the moment and stands back to look at her*) Ah—Oh-pay-gay-day, oh-gbah-mu-shay. (*A Yoruba exclamation for admiration*) You wear it well . . . very well . . . mutilated hair and all.

BENEATHA (*Turning suddenly*) My hair—what's wrong with my hair?

ASAGAI (*Shrugging*) Were you born with it like that?

BENEATHA (*Reaching up to touch it*) No . . . of course not.

(*She looks back to the mirror, disturbed*)

ASAGAI (*Smiling*) How then?

BENEATHA You know perfectly well how . . . as crinkly as yours . . . that's how.

ASAGAI And it is ugly to you that way?

BENEATHA (*Quickly*) Oh, no—not ugly . . . (*More slowly, apologetically*) But it's so hard to manage when it's, well—raw.

ASAGAI And so to accommodate that—you mutilate it every week?

BENEATHA It's not mutilation!

ASAGAI (*Laughing aloud at her seriousness*) Oh . . . please! I am only teasing you because you are so very serious about these things. (*He stands back from her and folds his arms across his chest as he watches her pulling at her hair and frowning in the mirror*) Do you remember the first time you met me at school? . . . (*He laughs*) You came up to me and you said—and I thought you were the most serious little thing I had ever seen—you said: (*He imitates her*) "Mr. Asagai—I want very much to talk with you. About Africa. You see, Mr. Asagai, I am looking for my *identity!*"

(*He laughs*)

BENEATHA (*Turning to him, not laughing*) Yes—

(*Her face is quizzical, profoundly disturbed*)

ASAGAI (*Still teasing and reaching out and taking her face in his hands and turning her profile to him*) Well . . . it is true that this is not so much a profile of a Hollywood queen as perhaps a queen of the Nile—(*A mock dismissal of the importance of the question*) But what does it matter? Assimilationism is so popular in your country.

BENEATHA (*Wheeling, passionately, sharply*) I am not an assimilationist!

ASAGAI (*The protest hangs in the room for a moment and* ASAGAI *studies her, his laughter fading*) Such a serious one. (*There is a pause*) So—you like the robes? You must take excellent care of them—they are from my sister's personal wardrobe.

BENEATHA (*With incredulity*) You—you sent all the way home—for me?

ASAGAI (*With charm*) For you—I would do much more . . . Well, that is what I came for. I must go.

BENEATHA Will you call me Monday?

ASAGAI Yes . . . We have a great deal to talk about. I mean about identity and time and all that.

BENEATHA Time?

ASAGAI Yes. About how much time one needs to know what one feels.

BENEATHA You see! You never understood that there is more than one kind of feeling which can exist between a man and a woman—or, at least, there should be.

ASAGAI (*Shaking his head negatively but gently*) No. Between a man and a woman there need be only one kind of feeling. I have that for you . . . Now even . . . right this moment . . .

BENEATHA I know—and by itself—it won't do. I can find that anywhere.

ASAGAI For a woman it should be enough.

BENEATHA I know—because that's what it says in all the novels that men write. But it isn't. Go ahead and laugh—but I'm not interested in being someone's little episode in America or—(*With feminine vengeance*)—one of them! (ASAGAI *has burst into laughter again*) That's funny as hell, huh!

ASAGAI It's just that every American girl I have known has said that to me. White—black—in this you are all the same. And the same speech, too!

BENEATHA (*Angrily*) Yuk, yuk, yuk!

ASAGAI It's how you can be sure that the world's most liberated women are not liberated at all. You all talk about it too much!

(MAMA *enters and is immediately all social charm because of the presence of a guest*)

BENEATHA Oh—Mama—this is Mr. Asagai.

MAMA How do you do?

ASAGAI (*Total politeness to an elder*) How do you do, Mrs. Younger. Please forgive me for coming at such an outrageous hour on a Saturday.

MAMA Well, you are quite welcome. I just hope you understand that our house don't always look like this. (*Chatterish*) You must come again. I would love to hear all about—(*Not sure of the name*)—your country. I think it's so sad the way our American Negroes don't know nothing about Africa 'cept Tarzan and all that. And all that money they pour into these churches when they ought to be helping you people over there drive out them French and Englishmen done taken away your land.

(*The mother flashes a slightly superior look at her daughter upon completion of the recitation*)

ASAGAI (*Taken aback by this sudden and acutely unrelated expression of sympathy*) Yes . . . yes . . .

MAMA (*Smiling at him suddenly and relaxing and looking him over*) How many miles is it from here to where you come from?

ASAGAI   Many thousands.

MAMA   (*Looking at him as she would* WALTER) I bet you don't half look after yourself, being away from your mama either. I spec you better come 'round here from time to time to get yourself some decent home-cooked meals . . .

ASAGAI   (*Moved*) Thank you. Thank you very much. (*They are all quiet, then—*) Well . . . I must go. I will call you Monday, Alaiyo.

MAMA   What's that he call you?

ASAGAI   Oh—"Alaiyo." I hope you don't mind. It is what you would call a nickname, I think. It is a Yoruba word. I am a Yoruba.

MAMA   (*Looking at* BENEATHA) I—I thought he was from—(*Uncertain*)

ASAGAI   (*Understanding*) Nigeria is my country. Yoruba is my tribal origin—

BENEATHA   You didn't tell us what Alaiyo means . . . for all I know, you might be calling me Little Idiot or something . . .

ASAGAI   Well . . . let me see . . . I do not know how just to explain it . . . The sense of a thing can be so different when it changes languages.

BENEATHA   You're evading.

ASAGAI   No—really it is difficult . . . (*Thinking*) It means . . . it means One for Whom Bread— Food—Is Not Enough. (*He looks at her*) Is that all right?

BENEATHA   (*Understanding, softly*) Thank you.

MAMA   (*Looking from one to the other and not understanding any of it*) Well . . . that's nice . . . You must come see us again—Mr.——

ASAGAI   Ah-sah-guy . . .

MAMA   Yes . . . Do come again

ASAGAI   Good-bye.

(*He exits*)

MAMA   (*After him*) Lord, that's a pretty thing just went out here! (*Insinuatingly, to her daughter*) Yes, I guess I see why we done commence to get so interested in Africa 'round here. Missionaries my aunt Jenny!

(*She exits*)

BENEATHA   Oh, Mama! . . .

(She picks up the Nigerian dress and holds it up to her in front of the mirror again. She sets the headdress on haphazardly and then notices her hair again and clutches at it and then replaces the headdress and frowns at herself. Then she starts to wriggle in front of the mirror as she thinks a Nigerian woman might. TRAVIS *enters and stands regarding her)*

TRAVIS   What's the matter, girl, you cracking up?

BENEATHA   Shut up.

(She pulls the headdress off and looks at herself in the mirror and clutches at her hair again and squinches her eyes as if trying to imagine something. Then, suddenly, she gets her raincoat and kerchief and hurriedly prepares for going out)

MAMA   *(Coming back into the room)* She's resting now. Travis, baby, run next door and ask Miss Johnson to please let me have a little kitchen cleanser. This here can is empty as Jacob's kettle.

TRAVIS   I just came in.

MAMA   Do as you told. *(He exits and she looks at her daughter)* Where you going?

BENEATHA   *(Halting at the door)* To become a queen of the Nile!

(She exits in a breathless blaze of glory. RUTH *appears in the bedroom doorway)*

MAMA   Who told you to get up?

RUTH   Ain't nothing wrong with me to be lying in no bed for. Where did Bennie go?

MAMA   *(Drumming her fingers)* Far as I could make out—to Egypt. *(RUTH just looks at her)* What time is it getting to?

RUTH   Ten twenty. And the mailman going to ring that bell this morning just like he done every morning for the last umpteen years.

(TRAVIS comes in with the cleanser can)

TRAVIS   She say to tell you that she don't have much.

MAMA   *(Angrily)* Lord, some people I could name sure is tight-fisted! *(Directing her grandson)* Mark two cans of cleanser down on the list there. If she that hard up for kitchen cleanser, I sure don't want to forget to get her none!

RUTH   Lena—maybe the woman is just short on cleanser—

MAMA (*Not listening*)—Much baking powder as she done borrowed from me all these years, she could of done gone into the baking business!

(*The bell sounds suddenly and sharply and all three are stunned—serious and silent—mid-speech. In spite of all the other conversations and distractions of the morning, this is what they have been waiting for, even* TRAVIS *who looks helplessly from his mother to his grandmother.* RUTH *is the first to come to life again*)

RUTH (*To* TRAVIS) Get down them steps, boy!

(TRAVIS *snaps to life and flies out to get the mail*)

MAMA (*Her eyes wide, her hand to her breast*) You mean it done really come?

RUTH (*Excited*) Oh, Miss Lena!

MAMA (*Collecting herself*) Well . . . I don't know what we all so excited about 'round here for. We known it was coming for months.

RUTH That's a whole lot different from having it come and being able to hold it in your hands . . . a piece of paper worth ten thousand dollars . . . (TRAVIS *bursts back into the room. He holds the envelope high above his head, like a little dancer, his face is radiant and he is breathless. He moves to his grandmother with sudden slow ceremony and puts the envelope into her hands. She accepts it, and then merely holds it and looks at it*) Come on! Open it . . . Lord have mercy, I wish Walter Lee was here!

TRAVIS Open it, Grandmama!

MAMA (*Staring at it*) Now you all be quiet. It's just a check.

RUTH Open it . . .

MAMA (*Still staring at it*) Now don't act silly . . . We ain't never been no people to act silly 'bout no money—

RUTH (*Swiftly*) We ain't never had none before—OPEN IT!

(MAMA *finally makes a good strong tear and pulls out the thin blue slice of paper and inspects it closely. The boy and his mother study it raptly over* MAMA'S *shoulders*)

MAMA Travis! (*She is counting off with doubt*) Is that the right number of zeros?

TRAVIS Yes'm . . . ten thousand dollars. Gaalee, Grandmama, you rich.

MAMA (*She holds the check away from her, still looking at it. Slowly her face sobers into a mask of unhappiness*) Ten thousand dollars. (*She hands it to*

RUTH) Put it away somewhere, Ruth. (*She does not look at* RUTH; *her eyes seem to be seeing something somewhere very far off*) Ten thousand dollars they give you. Ten thousand dollars.

TRAVIS   (*To his mother, sincerely*) What's the matter with Grandmama— don't she want to be rich?

RUTH   (*Distractedly*) You go on out and play now, baby. (TRAVIS *exits.* MAMA *starts wiping dishes absently, humming intently to herself.* RUTH *turns to her, with kind exasperation*) You've gone and got yourself upset.

MAMA   (*Not looking at her*) I spec if it wasn't for you all . . . I would just put that money away or give it to the church or something.

RUTH   Now what kind of talk is that. Mr. Younger would just be plain mad if he could hear you talking foolish like that.

MAMA   (*Stopping and staring off*) Yes . . . he sure would. (*Sighing*) We got enough to do with that money, all right. (*She halts then, and turns and looks at her daughter-in-law hard;* RUTH *avoids her eyes and* MAMA *wipes her hands with finality and starts to speak firmly to* RUTH) Where did you go today, girl?

RUTH   To the doctor.

MAMA   (*Impatiently*) Now, Ruth . . . you know better than that. Old Doctor Jones is strange enough in his way but there ain't nothing 'bout him make somebody slip and call him "she"—like you done this morning.

RUTH   Well, that's what happened—my tongue slipped.

MAMA   You went to see that woman, didn't you?

RUTH   (*Defensively, giving herself away*) What woman you talking about?

MAMA   (*Angrily*) That woman who—

(WALTER *enters in great excitement*)

WALTER   Did it come?

MAMA   (*Quietly*) Can't you give people a Christian greeting before you start asking about money?

WALTER   (*To* RUTH) Did it come? (RUTH *unfolds the check and lays it quietly before him, watching him intently with thoughts of her own.* WALTER *sits down and grasps it close and counts off the zeros*) Ten thousand dollars— (*He turns suddenly, frantically to his mother and draws some papers out of his breast pocket*) Mama—look. Old Willy Harris put everything on paper—

MAMA Son—I think you ought to talk to your wife . . . I'll go out and leave you alone if you want—

WALTER I can talk to her later—Mama, look—

MAMA Son—

WALTER WILL SOMEBODY PLEASE LISTEN TO ME TODAY!

MAMA (*Quietly*) I don't 'low no yellin' in this house, Walter Lee, and you know it—(WALTER *stares at them in frustration and starts to speak several times*) And there ain't going to be no investing in no liquor stores.

WALTER But, Mama, you ain't even looked at it.

MAMA I don't aim to have to speak on that again.

(*A long pause*)

WALTER You ain't looked at it and you don't aim to have to speak on that again? You ain't even looked at it and *you* have decided—(*Crumpling his papers*) Well, *you* tell that to my boy tonight when you put him to sleep on the living-room couch . . . (*Turning to* MAMA *and speaking directly to her*) Yeah—and tell it to my wife, Mama, tomorrow when she has to go out of here to look after somebody else's kids. And tell it to *me*, Mama, every time we need a new pair of curtains and I have to watch you go out and work in somebody's kitchen. Yeah, you tell me then!

(WALTER *starts out*)

RUTH Where you going?

WALTER I'm going out!

RUTH Where?

WALTER Just out of this house somewhere—

RUTH (*Getting her coat*) I'll come too.

WALTER I don't want you to come!

RUTH I got something to talk to you about, Walter.

WALTER That's too bad.

MAMA (*Still quietly*) Walter Lee—(*She waits and he finally turns and looks at her*) Sit down.

WALTER I'm a grown man, Mama.

MAMA Ain't nobody said you wasn't grown. But you still in my house and my presence. And as long as you are—you'll talk to your wife civil. Now sit down.

RUTH (*Suddenly*) Oh, let him go on out and drink himself to death! He makes me sick to my stomach! (*She flings her coat against him and exits to bedroom*)

WALTER (*Violently flinging the coat after her*) And you turn mine too, baby! (*The door slams behind her*) That was my biggest mistake—

MAMA (*Still quietly*) Walter, what is the matter with you?

WALTER Matter with me? Ain't nothing the matter with *me*!

MAMA Yes there is. Something eating you up like a crazy man. Something more than me not giving you this money. The past few years I been watching it happen to you. You get all nervous acting and kind of wild in the eyes—(WALTER *jumps up impatiently at her words*) I said sit there now, I'm talking to you!

WALTER Mama—I don't need no nagging at me today.

MAMA Seem like you getting to a place where you always tied up in some kind of knot about something. But if anybody ask you 'bout it you just yell at 'em and bust out the house and go out and drink somewheres. Walter Lee, people can't live with that. Ruth's a good, patient girl in her way—but you getting to be too much. Boy, don't make the mistake of driving that girl away from you.

WALTER Why—what she do for me?

MAMA She loves you.

WALTER Mama—I'm going out. I want to go off somewhere and be by myself for a while.

MAMA I'm sorry 'bout your liquor store, son. It just wasn't the thing for us to do. That's what I want to tell you about—

WALTER I got to go out, Mama—

(*He rises*)

MAMA It's dangerous, son.

WALTER What's dangerous?

MAMA When a man goes outside his home to look for peace.

WALTER (*Beseechingly*) Then why can't there never be no peace in this house then?

MAMA You done found it in some other house?

WALTER No—there ain't no woman! Why do women always think there's a woman somewhere when a man gets restless. (*Picks up the check*) Do you know what this money means to me? Do you know what this money can do for us? (*Puts it back*) Mama—Mama—I want so many things . . .

MAMA Yes, son—

WALTER I want so many things that they are driving me kind of crazy . . . Mama—look at me.

MAMA I'm looking at you. You a good-looking boy. You got a job, a nice wife, a fine boy and—

WALTER A job. (*Looks at her*) Mama, a job? I open and close car doors all day long. I drive a man around in his limousine and I say, "Yes, sir; no, sir; very good, sir; shall I take the Drive, sir?" Mama, that ain't no kind of job . . . that ain't nothing at all. (*Very quietly*) Mama, I don't know if I can make you understand.

MAMA Understand what, baby?

WALTER (*Quietly*) Sometimes it's like I can see the future stretched out in front of me—just plain as day. The future, Mama. Hanging over there at the edge of my days. Just waiting for me—a big, looming blank space—full of *nothing*. Just waiting for *me*. But it don't have to be. (*Pause. Kneeling beside her chair*) Mama—sometimes when I'm downtown and I pass them cool, quiet-looking restaurants where them white boys are sitting back and talking 'bout things . . . sitting there turning deals worth millions of dollars . . . sometimes I see guys don't look much older than me—

MAMA Son—how come you talk so much 'bout money?

WALTER (*With immense passion*) Because it is life, Mama!

MAMA (*Quietly*) Oh—(*Very quietly*) So now it's life. Money is life. Once upon a time freedom used to be life—now it's money. I guess the world really do change . . .

WALTER No—it was always money, Mama. We just didn't know about it.

MAMA No . . . something has changed. (*She looks at him*) You are something new, boy. In my time we was worried about not being lynched and getting to the North if we could and how to stay alive and still have a pinch of dignity too . . . Now here come you and Beneatha—talking 'bout things we ain't never even thought about hardly, me and your daddy. You ain't satisfied or proud of nothing we done. I mean that you had a home; that we kept you out of trouble till you was grown; that you don't have to ride to work on the back of nobody's streetcar—You my children—but how different we done become.

WALTER (*A long beat. He pats her hand and gets up*) You just don't understand, Mama, you just don't understand.

MAMA Son—do you know your wife is expecting another baby? (WALTER *stands, stunned, and absorbs what his mother has said*) That's what she wanted to talk to you about. (WALTER *sinks down into a chair*) This ain't for me to be telling—but you ought to know. (*She waits*) I think Ruth is thinking 'bout getting rid of that child.

WALTER (*Slowly understanding*) No—no—Ruth wouldn't do that.

MAMA When the world gets ugly enough—a woman will do anything for her family. *The part that's already living.*

WALTER You don't know Ruth, Mama, if you think she would do that.

(RUTH *opens the bedroom door and stands there a little limp*)

RUTH (*Beaten*) Yes I would too, Walter. (*Pause*) I gave her a five dollar down payment.

(*There is total silence as the man stares at his wife and the mother stares at her son*)

MAMA (*Presently*) Well—(*Tightly*) Well—son, I'm waiting to hear you say something . . . (*She waits*) I'm waiting to hear how you be your father's son. Be the man he was . . . (*Pause. The silence shouts*) Your wife say she going to destroy your child. And I'm waiting to hear you talk like him and say we a people who give children life, not who destroys them— (*She rises*) I'm waiting to see you stand up and look like your daddy and say we done give up one baby to poverty and that we ain't going to give up nary another one . . . I'm waiting.

WALTER Ruth—(*He can say nothing*)

MAMA If you a son of mine, tell her! (WALTER *picks up his keys and his coat and walks out. She continues, bitterly*) You . . . you are a disgrace to your father's memory. Somebody get me my hat!

Curtain

Act II

Time: Later the same day.

At rise: RUTH *is ironing again. She has the radio going. Presently* BENEATHA'S *bedroom door opens and* RUTH'S *mouth falls and she puts the iron down in fascination.*

RUTH What have we got on tonight!

BENEATHA *(Emerging grandly from the doorway so that we can see her thoroughly robed in the costume* ASAGAI *brought)* You are looking at what a well-dressed Nigerian woman wears—*(She parades for* RUTH, *with her hair completely hidden by the headdress; she is coquettishly fanning herself with an ornate oriental fan, mistakenly more like Butterfly than any Nigerian that ever was)* Isn't it beautiful? *(She promenades to the radio and, with an arrogant flourish, turns off the good loud blues that is playing)* Enough of this assimilationist junk! *(*RUTH *follows her with her eyes as she goes to the phonograph and puts on a record and turns and waits ceremoniously for the music to come up. Then, with a shout—)* OCOMOGOSIAY!

*(*RUTH *jumps. The music comes up, a lovely Nigerian melody.* BENEATHA *listens, enraptured, her eyes far away—"back to the past." She begins to dance.* RUTH *is dumbfounded)*

RUTH What kind of dance is that?

BENEATHA A folk dance.

RUTH *(Pearl Bailey)* What kind of folks do that, honey?

BENEATHA It's from Nigeria. It's a dance of welcome.

RUTH Who are you welcoming?

BENEATHA The men back to the village.

RUTH Where they been?

BENEATHA How should I know—out hunting or something. Anyway, they are coming back now . . .

RUTH Well, that's good.

BENEATHA (*With the record*)
Alundi, alundi
Alundi alunya
Jop pu a jeepua
Ang gu sooooooooo

Ai yai yae . . .
Ayehaye—alundi . . .

(WALTER *comes in during this performance; he has obviously been drinking. He leans against the door heavily and watches his sister, at first with distaste. Then his eyes look off—"back to the past"—as he lifts both his fists to the roof, screaming*)

WALTER YEAH . . . AND ETHIOPIA STRETCH FORTH HER HANDS AGAIN! . . .

RUTH (*Drily, looking at him*) Yes—and Africa sure is claiming her own tonight. (*She gives them both up and starts ironing again*)

WALTER (*All in a drunken, dramatic shout*) Shut up! . . . I'm digging them drums . . . then drums move me! . . . (*He makes his weaving way to his wife's face and leans in close to her*) In my *heart of hearts*—(*He thumps his chest*)—I am much warrior!

RUTH (*Without even looking up*) In your heart of hearts you are much drunkard.

WALTER (*Coming away from her and starting to wander around the room, shouting*) Me and Jomo . . . (*Intently, in his sister's face. She has stopped dancing to watch him in this unknown mood*) That's my man, Kenyatta. (*Shouting and thumping his chest*) FLAMING SPEAR! HOT DAMN! (*He is suddenly in possession of an imaginary spear and actively spearing enemies all over the room*) OCOMOGOSIAY . . .

BENEATHA (*To encourage* WALTER, *thoroughly caught up with this side of him*) OCOMOGOSIAY, FLAMING SPEAR!

WALTER THE LION IS WAKING . . . OWIMOWEH!

(*He pulls his shirt open and leaps up on the table and gestures with his spear*)

BENEATHA OWIMOWEH!

WALTER (*On the table, very far gone, his eyes pure glass sheets. He sees what we cannot, that he is a leader of his people, a great chief, a descendant of Chaka, and that the hour to march has come*) Listen, my black brothers—

BENEATHA OCOMOGOSIAY!

WALTER —Do you hear the waters rushing against the shores of the coast-lands—

BENEATHA OCOMOGOSIAY!

WALTER —Do you hear the screeching of the cocks in yonder hills beyond where the chiefs meet in council for the coming of the mighty war—

BENEATHA OCOMOGOSIAY!

(*And now the lighting shifts subtly to suggest the world of* WALTER'S *imagination, and the mood shifts from pure comedy. It is the inner* WALTER *speaking: the Southside chauffeur has assumed an unexpected majesty*)

WALTER —Do you hear the beating of the wings of the birds flying low over the mountains and the low places of our land—

BENEATHA OCOMOGOSIAY!

WALTER —Do you hear the singing of the women, singing the war songs of our fathers to the babies in the great houses? Singing the sweet war songs! (*The doorbell rings*) OH, DO YOU HEAR, MY BLACK BROTHERS!

BENEATHA (*Completely gone*) We hear you, Flaming Spear—

(RUTH *shuts off the phonograph and opens the door.* GEORGE MURCHISON *enters*)

WALTER Telling us to prepare for the GREATNESS OF THE TIME! (*Lights back to normal. He turns and sees* GEORGE) Black Brother!

(*He extends his hand for the fraternal clasp*)

GEORGE Black Brother, hell!

RUTH (*Having had enough, and embarrassed for the whole family*) Beneatha, you got company—what's the matter with you? Walter Lee Younger, get down off that table and stop acting like a fool . . .

(WALTER *comes down off the table suddenly and makes a quick exit to the bathroom*)

RUTH He's had a little to drink . . . I don't know what her excuse is.

GEORGE (*To* BENEATHA) Look honey, we're going *to* the theatre—we're not going to be *in* it . . . so go change, huh?

(BENEATHA *looks at him and slowly, ceremoniously, lifts her hands and pulls off the headdress. Her hair is close-cropped and unstraightened.* GEORGE *freezes mid-sentence and* RUTH'S *eyes all but fan out of her head*)

GEORGE What in the name of—

RUTH (*Touching* BENEATHA'S *hair*) Girl, you done lost your natural mind!? Look at your head!

GEORGE What have you done to your head—I mean your hair!

BENEATHA Nothing—except cut it off.

RUTH Now that's the truth—it's what ain't been done to it! You expect this boy to go out with you with your head all nappy like that?

BENEATHA (*Looking at* GEORGE) That's up to George. If he's ashamed of his heritage—

GEORGE Oh, don't be so proud of yourself, Bennie—just because you look eccentric.

BENEATHA How can something that's natural be eccentric?

GEORGE That's what being eccentric means—being natural. Get dressed.

BENEATHA I don't like that, George.

RUTH Why must you and your brother make an argument out of everything people say?

BENEATHA Because I hate assimilationist Negroes!

RUTH Will somebody please tell me what assimila-whoever means!

GEORGE Oh, it's just a college girl's way of calling people Uncle Toms—but that isn't what it means at all.

RUTH Well, what does it mean?

BENEATHA (*Cutting* GEORGE *off and staring at him as she replies to* RUTH) It means someone who is willing to give up his own culture and submerge himself completely in the dominant, and in this case *oppressive* culture!

GEORGE Oh, dear, dear, dear! Here we go again! A lecture on the African past! On our Great West African Heritage! In one second we will hear all about the great Ashanti empires; the great Songhay civilizations; and the great sculpture of Bénin—and then some poetry in the Bantu—and the whole monologue will end with the word *heritage!* (*Nastily*) Let's face it, baby, your heritage is nothing but a bunch of raggedy-assed spirituals and some grass huts!

BENEATHA GRASS HUTS! (RUTH *crosses to her and forcibly pushes her toward the bedroom*) See there . . . you are standing there in your splendid ignorance talking about people who were the first to smelt iron on the face of the earth! (RUTH *is pushing her through the door*) The Ashanti were performing surgical operations when the English—(RUTH *pulls the door to, with* BENEATHA *on the other side, and smiles graciously at* GEORGE. BENEATHA *opens the door and shouts the end of the sentence defiantly at* GEORGE)—were still tattooing themselves with blue dragons! (*She goes back inside*)

RUTH Have a seat, George (*They both sit.* RUTH *folds her hands rather primly on her lap, determined to demonstrate the civilization of the family*) Warm, ain't it? I mean for September. (*Pause*) Just like they always say about Chicago weather: If it's too hot or cold for you, just wait a minute and it'll change. (*She smiles happily at this cliché of clichés*) Everybody says it's got to do with them bombs and things they keep setting off. (*Pause*) Would you like a nice cold beer?

GEORGE No, thank you. I don't care for beer. (*He looks at his watch*) I hope she hurries up.

RUTH What time is the show?

GEORGE It's an eight-thirty curtain. That's just Chicago, though. In New York standard curtain time is eight forty.

(*He is rather proud of this knowledge*)

RUTH (*Properly appreciating it*) You get to New York a lot?

GEORGE (*Offhand*) Few times a year.

RUTH Oh—that's nice. I've never been to New York.

(WALTER *enters. We feel he has relieved himself, but the edge of unreality is still with him*)

WALTER New York ain't got nothing Chicago ain't. Just a bunch of hustling people all squeezed up together—being "Eastern."

(*He turns his face into a screw of displeasure*)

GEORGE Oh—you've been?

WALTER *Plenty of times.*

RUTH (*Shocked at the lie*) Walter Lee Younger!

WALTER (*Staring her down*) Plenty! (*Pause*) What we got to drink in this house? Why don't you offer this man some refreshment. (*To George*) They don't know how to entertain people in this house, man.

GEORGE Thank you—I don't really care for anything.

WALTER (*Feeling his head; sobriety coming*) Where's Mama?

RUTH She ain't come back yet.

WALTER (*Looking* MURCHISON *over from head to toe, scrutinizing his carefully casual tweed sports jacket over cashmere V-neck sweater over soft eyelet shirt and tie, and soft slacks, finished off with white buckskin shoes*) Why all you college boys wear them faggoty-looking white shoes?

RUTH Walter Lee!

(GEORGE MURCHISON *ignores the remark*)

WALTER (*To* RUTH) Well, they look crazy as hell—white shoes, cold as it is.

RUTH (*Crushed*) You have to excuse him—

WALTER No he don't! Excuse me for what? What you always excusing me for! I'll excuse myself when I needs to be excused! (*A pause*) They look as funny as them black knee socks Beneatha wears out of here all the time.

RUTH It's the college *style*, Walter.

WALTER Style, hell. She looks like she got burnt legs or something!

RUTH Oh, Walter—

WALTER (*An irritable mimic*) Oh, Walter! Oh Walter! (*To* MURCHISON) How's your old man making out? I understand you all going to buy that big hotel on the Drive? (*He finds a beer in the refrigerator, wanders over to* MURCHISON, *sipping and wiping his lips with the back of his hand, and straddling a chair backwards to talk to the other man*) Shrewd move. Your old man is all right, man. (*Tapping his head and half winking for emphasis*) I mean he knows how to operate. I mean he thinks *big*, you know what I mean, I mean for a *home*, you know? But I think he's kind of running out of ideas now. I'd like to talk to him. Listen, man, I got some plans that could turn this city upside down. I mean think like he does. *Big*. Invest big, gamble big, hell, lose *big* if you have to, you know what I mean. It's hard to find a man on this whole Southside who understands my kind of thinking—you dig? (*He scrutinizes* MURCHISON *again, drinks his beer, squints his eyes and leans in close, confidential, man to man)* Me and you ought to sit down and talk sometimes, man. Man, I got me some ideas . . .

GEORGE   *(With boredom)* Yeah—sometimes we'll have to do that, Walter.

WALTER   *(Understanding the indifference, and offended)* Yeah—well, when you get the time, man. I know you a busy little boy.

RUTH   Walter, please—

WALTER   *(Bitterly, hurt)* I know ain't nothing in this world as busy as you colored college boys with your fraternity pins and white shoes . . .

RUTH   *(Covering her face with humiliation)* Oh, Walter Lee—

WALTER   I see you all all the time—with the books tucked under your arms—going to your *(British A—a mimic)* "clahsses." And for what! What the hell you learning over there? Filling up your heads—*(Counting off on his fingers)*—with the sociology and the psychology—but they teaching you how to be a man? How to take over and run the world? They teaching you how to run a rubber plantation or a steel mill? Naw—just to talk proper and read books and wear them faggoty-looking white shoes . . .

GEORGE   *(Looking at him with distaste, a little above it all)* You're all wacked up with bitterness, man.

WALTER   *(Intently, almost quietly, between the teeth, glaring at the boy)* And you—ain't you bitter, man? Ain't you just about had it yet? Don't you see no stars gleaming that you can't reach out and grab? You happy?— You contented son-of-a-bitch—you happy? You got it made? Bitter? Man, I'm a volcano. Bitter? Here I am a giant—surrounded by ants! Ants who can't even understand what it is the giant is talking about.

RUTH   *(Passionately and suddenly)* Oh, Walter—ain't you with nobody!

WALTER   *(Violently)* No! 'Cause ain't nobody with me! Not even my own mother!

RUTH   Walter, that's a terrible thing to say!

(BENEATHA enters, dressed for the evening in a cocktail dress and earrings, hair natural)

GEORGE   Well—hey—*(Crosses to BENEATHA; thoughtful, with emphasis, since this is a reversal)* You look great!

WALTER (*Seeing his sister's hair for the first time*) What's the matter with your head?

BENEATHA (*Tired of the jokes now*) I cut it off, Brother.

WALTER (*Coming close to inspect it and walking around her*) Well, I'll be damned. So that's what they mean by the African bush . . .

BENEATHA Ha ha. Let's go, George.

GEORGE (*Looking at her*) You know something? I like it. It's sharp. I mean it really is. (*Helps her into her wrap*)

RUTH Yes—I think so, too. (*She goes to the mirror and starts to clutch at her hair*)

WALTER Oh no! You leave yours alone, baby. You might turn out to have a pin-shaped head or something!

BENEATHA See you all later.

RUTH Have a nice time.

GEORGE Thanks. Good night. (*Half out the door, he re-opens it. To* WALTER) Good night, Prometheus!

(BENEATHA *and* GEORGE *exit*)

WALTER (*To* RUTH) Who is Prometheus?

RUTH I don't know. Don't worry about it.

WALTER (*In a fury, pointing after* GEORGE) See there—they get to a point where they can't insult you man to man—they got to go talk about something ain't nobody ever heard of!

RUTH How do you know it was an insult? (*To humor him*) Maybe Prometheus is a nice fellow.

WALTER Prometheus! I bet there ain't even no such thing! I bet that simple-minded clown—

RUTH Walter—

(*She stops what she is doing and looks at him*)

WALTER (*Yelling*) Don't start!

RUTH Start what?

WALTER Your nagging! Where was I? Who was I with? How much money did I spend?

RUTH *(Plaintively)* Walter Lee—why don't we just try to talk about it . . .

WALTER *(Not listening)* I been out talking with people who understand me. People who care about the things I got on my mind.

RUTH *(Wearily)* I guess that means people like Willy Harris.

WALTER Yes, people like Willy Harris.

RUTH *(With a sudden flash of impatience)* Why don't you all just hurry up and go into the banking business and stop talking about it!

WALTER Why? You want to know why? 'Cause we all tied up in a race of people that don't know how to do nothing but moan, pray and have babies!

(The line is too bitter even for him and he looks at her and sits down)

RUTH Oh, Walter . . . *(Softly)* Honey, why can't you stop fighting me?

WALTER *(Without thinking)* Who's fighting you? Who even cares about you?

(This line begins the retardation of his mood)

RUTH Well—*(She waits a long time, and then with resignation starts to put away her things)* I guess I might as well go on to bed . . . *(More or less to herself)* I don't know where we lost it . . . but we have . . . *(Then, to him)* I—I'm sorry about this new baby, Walter. I guess maybe I better go on and do what I started . . . I guess I just didn't realize how bad things was with us . . . I guess I just didn't really realize—*(She starts out to the bedroom and stops)* You want some hot milk?

WALTER Hot milk?

RUTH Yes—hot milk.

WALTER Why hot milk?

RUTH 'Cause after all that liquor you come home with you ought to have something hot in your stomach.

WALTER I don't want no milk.

RUTH You want some coffee then?

WALTER No, I don't want no coffee. I don't want nothing hot to drink. *(Almost plaintively)* Why you always trying to give me something to eat?

RUTH *(Standing and looking at him helplessly)* What else can I give you, Walter Lee Younger?

(She stands and looks at him and presently turns to go out again. He lifts his head and watches her going away from him in a mood which began to emerge when he asked her "Who cares about you?")

WALTER It's been rough, ain't it, baby? *(She hears and stops but does not turn around and he continues to her back)* I guess between two people there ain't never as much understood as folks generally think there is. I mean like between me and you—*(She turns to face him)* How we gets to the place where we scared to talk softness to each other. *(He waits, thinking hard himself)* Why you think it got to be like that? *(He is thoughtful, almost as a child would be)* Ruth, what is it gets into people ought to be close?

RUTH I don't know, honey. I think about it a lot.

WALTER On account of you and me, you mean? The way things are with us. The way something done come down between us.

RUTH There ain't so much between us, Walter . . . Not when you come to me and try to talk to me. Try to be with me . . . a little even.

WALTER *(Total honesty)* Sometimes . . . sometimes . . . I don't even know how to try.

RUTH Walter—

WALTER Yes?

RUTH *(Coming to him, gently and with misgiving, but coming to him)* Honey . . . life don't have to be like this. I mean sometimes people can do things so that things are better . . . You remember how we used to talk when Travis was born . . . about the way we were going to live . . . the kind of house . . . *(She is stroking his head)* Well, it's all starting to slip away from us . . .

(He turns her to him and they look at each other and kiss, tenderly and hungrily. The door opens and MAMA enters—WALTER breaks away and jumps up. A beat)

WALTER Mama, where have you been?

MAMA My—them steps is longer than they used to be. Whew! *(She sits down and ignores him)* How you feeling this evening, Ruth?

(RUTH shrugs, disturbed at having been interrupted and watching her husband knowingly)

WALTER Mama, where have you been all day?

MAMA (*Still ignoring him and leaning on the table and changing to more comfortable shoes*) Where's Travis?

RUTH I let him go out earlier and he ain't come back yet. Boy, is he going to get it!

WALTER Mama!

MAMA (*As if she has heard him for the first time*) Yes, son?

WALTER Where did you go this afternoon?

MAMA I went downtown to tend to some business that I had to tend to.

WALTER What kind of business?

MAMA You know better than to question me like a child, Brother.

WALTER (*Rising and bending over the table*) Where were you, Mama? (*Bringing his fists down and shouting*) Mama, you didn't go do something with that insurance money, something crazy?

(*The front door opens slowly, interrupting him, and* TRAVIS *peeks his head in, less than hopefully*)

TRAVIS (*To his mother*) Mama, I—

RUTH "Mama I" nothing! You're going to get it, boy! Get on in that bedroom and get yourself ready!

TRAVIS But I—

MAMA Why don't you all never let the child explain hisself.

RUTH Keep out of it now, Lena.

(MAMA *clamps her lips together, and* RUTH *advances toward her son menacingly*)

RUTH A thousand times I have told you not to go off like that—

MAMA (*Holding out her arms to her grandson*) Well—at least let me tell him something. I want him to be the first one to hear . . . Come here, Travis. (*The boy obeys, gladly*) Travis—(*She takes him by the shoulder and looks into his face*)—you know that money we got in the mail this morning?

TRAVIS Yes'm—

MAMA Well—what you think your grandmama gone and done with that money?

TRAVIS I don't know, Grandmama.

MAMA (*Putting her fingers on his nose for emphasis*) She went out and she bought you a house! (*The explosion comes from* WALTER *at the end of the revelation and he jumps up and turns away from all of them in a fury.* MAMA *continues to* TRAVIS) You glad about the house? It's going to be yours when you get to be a man.

TRAVIS Yeah—I always wanted to live in a house.

MAMA All right, gimme some sugar then—(TRAVIS *puts his arms around her neck as she watches her son over the boy's shoulder. Then, to* TRAVIS, *after the embrace*) Now when you say your prayers tonight, you thank God and your grandfather—'cause it was him who give you the house—in his way.

RUTH (*Taking the boy from* MAMA *and pushing him toward the bedroom*) Now you get out of here and get ready for your beating.

TRAVIS Aw, Mama—

RUTH Get on in there—(*Closing the door behind him and turning radiantly to her mother-in-law*) So you went and did it!

MAMA (*Quietly, looking at her son with pain*) Yes, I did.

RUTH (*Raising both arms classically*) PRAISE GOD! (*Looks at* WALTER *a moment, who says nothing. She crosses rapidly to her husband*) Please, honey—let me be glad . . . you be glad too. (*She has laid her hands on his shoulders, but he shakes himself free of her roughly, without turning to face her*) Oh Walter . . . a home . . . a home. (*She comes back to* MAMA) Well—where is it? How big is it? How much it going to cost?

MAMA Well—

RUTH When we moving?

MAMA (*Smiling at her*) First of the month.

RUTH (*Throwing back her head with jubilance*) Praise God!

MAMA (*Tentatively, still looking at her son's back turned against her and* RUTH) It's—it's a nice house too . . . (*She cannot help speaking directly to him. An imploring quality in her voice, her manner, makes her almost like a girl now*) Three bedrooms—nice big one for you and Ruth . . . Me and Beneatha still have to share our room, but Travis have one of his own—and (*With difficulty*) I figure if the—new baby—is a boy, we could get one them double-decker outfits . . . And there's a yard with a little patch of dirt where I could maybe get to grow me a few flowers . . . And a nice big basement . . .

RUTH Walter honey, be glad—

MAMA (*Still to his back, fingering things on the table*) 'Course I don't want to make it sound fancier than it is . . . It's just a plain little old house—but it's made good and solid—and it will be *ours*. Walter Lee—it makes a difference in a man when he can walk around on floors that belong to him . . .

RUTH Where is it?

MAMA (*Frightened at this telling*) Well—well—it's out there in Clybourne Park—

(RUTH'S *radiance fades abruptly, and* WALTER *finally turns slowly to face his mother with incredulity and hostility*)

RUTH Where?

MAMA (*Matter-of-factly*) Four o six Clybourne Street, Clybourne Park.

RUTH Clybourne Park? Mama, there ain't no colored people living in Clybourne Park.

MAMA (*Almost idiotically*) Well, I guess there's going to be some now.

WALTER (*Bitterly*) So that's the peace and comfort you went out and bought for us today!

MAMA (*Raising her eyes to meet his finally*) Son—I just tried to find the nicest place for the least amount of money for my family.

RUTH (*Trying to recover from the shock*) Well—well—'course I ain't one never been 'fraid of no crackers, mind you—but—well, wasn't there no other houses nowhere?

MAMA Them houses they put up for colored in them areas way out all seem to cost twice as much as other houses. I did the best I could.

RUTH (*Struck senseless with the news, in its various degrees of goodness and trouble, she sits a moment, her fists propping her chin in thought, and then she starts to rise, bringing her fists down with vigor, the radiance spreading from cheek to cheek again*) Well—well!—All I can say is—if this is my time in life—MY TIME—to say good-bye—(*And she builds with momentum as she starts to circle the room with an exuberant, almost tearfully happy release*)—to these goddamned cracking walls!—(*She pounds the walls*)—and these marching roaches!—(*She wipes at an imaginary army of marching roaches*)—and this cramped little closet which ain't now or never was no kitchen! . . . then I say it loud and good, HALLELUJAH! AND

GOOD-BYE MISERY . . . I DON'T NEVER WANT TO SEE YOUR
UGLY FACE AGAIN! (*She laughs joyously, having practically destroyed
the apartment, and flings her arms up and lets them come down happily,
slowly, reflectively, over her abdomen, aware for the first time perhaps that
the life therein pulses with happiness and not despair*) Lena?

MAMA   (*Moved, watching her happiness*) Yes, honey?

RUTH   (*Looking off*) Is there—is there a whole lot of sunlight?

MAMA   (*Understanding*) Yes, child, there's a whole lot of sunlight.

(*Long pause*)

RUTH   (*Collecting herself and going to the door of the room* TRAVIS *is in*) Well—
I guess I better see 'bout Travis. (*To* MAMA) Lord, I sure don't feel like
whipping nobody today!

(*She exits*)

MAMA   (*The mother and son are left alone now and the mother waits a long
time, considering deeply, before she speaks*) Son—you—you understand
what I done, don't you? (WALTER *is silent and sullen*) I—I just seen my
family falling apart today . . . just falling to pieces in front of my eyes . . .
We couldn't of gone on like we was today. We was going backwards
'stead of forwards—talking 'bout killing babies and wishing each other
was dead . . . When it gets like that in life—you just got to do something
different, push on out and do something bigger . . . (*She waits*) I wish you
say something, son . . . I wish you'd say how deep inside you you think I
done the right thing—

WALTER   (*Crossing slowly to his bedroom door and finally turning there and
speaking measuredly*) What you need me to say you done right for? You
the head of this family. You run our lives like you want to. It was your
money and you did what you wanted with it. So what you need for me to
say it was all right for? (*Bitterly, to hurt her as deeply as he knows is possible*)
So you butchered up a dream of mine—you—who always talking 'bout
your children's dreams . . .

MAMA   Walter Lee—

(*He just closes the door behind him.* MAMA *sits alone, thinking heavily*)

Curtain

SCENE TWO

Time: Friday night. A few weeks later.

At rise: Packing crates mark the intention of the family move. BENEATHA *and* GEORGE *come in, presumably from an evening out again.*

GEORGE   O.K. . . . O.K., whatever you say . . . (*They both sit on the couch. He tries to kiss her. She moves away*) Look, we've had a nice evening; let's not spoil it, huh? . . .

(*He again turns her head and tries to nuzzle in and she turns away from him, not with distaste but with momentary lack of interest; in a mood to pursue what they were talking about*)

BENEATHA   I'm *trying* to talk to you.

GEORGE   We always talk.

BENEATHA   Yes—and I love to talk.

GEORGE   (*Exasperated; rising*) I know it and I don't mind it sometimes . . . I want you to cut it out, see—The moody stuff, I mean. I don't like it. You're a nice-looking girl . . . all over. That's all you need, honey, forget the atmosphere. Guys aren't going to go for the atmosphere—they're going to go for what they see. Be glad for that. Drop the Garbo routine. It doesn't go with you. As for myself, I want a nice—(*Groping*)—simple (*Thoughtfully*)—sophisticated girl . . . not a poet—O.K.?

(*He starts to kiss her, she rebuffs him again and he jumps up*)

BENEATHA   Why are you angry, George?

GEORGE   Because this is stupid! I don't go out with you to discuss the nature of "quiet desperation" or to hear all about your thoughts—because the world will go on thinking what it thinks regardless—

BENEATHA   Then why read books? Why go to school?

GEORGE   (*With artificial patience, counting on his fingers*) It's simple. You read books—to learn facts—to get grades—to pass the course—to get a degree. That's all—it has nothing to do with thoughts.

(*A long pause*)

BENEATHA   I see. (*He starts to sit*) Good night, George.

(GEORGE *looks at her a little oddly, and starts to exit. He meets* MAMA *coming in*)

GEORGE Oh—hello, Mrs. Younger.

MAMA Hello, George, how you feeling?

GEORGE Fine—fine, how are you?

MAMA Oh, a little tired. You know them steps can get you after a day's work. You all have a nice time tonight?

GEORGE Yes—a fine time. A fine time.

MAMA Well, good night.

GEORGE Good night. (*He exits.* MAMA *closes the door behind her*) Hello, honey. What you sitting like that for?

BENEATHA I'm just sitting.

MAMA Didn't you have a nice time?

BENEATHA No.

MAMA No? What's the matter?

BENEATHA Mama, George is a fool—honest. (*She rises*)

MAMA (*Hustling around unloading the packages she has entered with. She stops*) Is he, baby?

BENEATHA Yes.

(BENEATHA *makes up* TRAVIS' *bed as she talks*)

MAMA You sure?

BENEATHA Yes.

MAMA Well—I guess you better not waste your time with no fools.

(BENEATHA *looks up at her mother, watching her put groceries in the refrigerator. Finally she gathers up her things and starts into the bedroom. At the door she stops and looks back at her mother*)

BENEATHA Mama—

MAMA Yes, baby—

BENEATHA Thank you.

MAMA For what?

BENEATHA For understanding me this time.

(She exits quickly and the mother stands, smiling a little, looking at the place where BENEATHA *just stood.* RUTH *enters)*

RUTH Now don't you fool with any of this stuff, Lena—

MAMA Oh, I just thought I'd sort a few things out. Is Brother here?

RUTH Yes.

MAMA *(With concern)* Is he—

RUTH *(Reading her eyes)* Yes.

*(*MAMA *is silent and someone knocks on the door.* MAMA *and* RUTH *exchange weary and knowing glances and* RUTH *opens it to admit the neighbor,* MRS. JOHNSON, *who is a rather squeaky wide-eyed lady of no particular age, with a newspaper under her arm)*

MAMA *(Changing her expression to acute delight and a ringing cheerful greeting)* Oh—hello there, Johnson.

JOHNSON *(This is a woman who decided long ago to be enthusiastic about EVERYTHING in life and she is inclined to wave her wrist vigorously at the height of her exclamatory comments)* Hello there, yourself! H'you this evening, Ruth?

RUTH *(Not much of a deceptive type)* Fine, Mis' Johnson, h'you?

JOHNSON Fine. *(Reaching out quickly, playfully, and patting* RUTH'S *stomach)* Ain't you starting to poke out none yet! *(She mugs with delight at the over-familiar remark and her eyes dart around looking at the crates and packing preparation;* MAMA's *face is a cold sheet of endurance)* Oh, ain't we getting ready 'round here, though! Yessir! Lookathere! I'm telling you the Youngers is really getting ready to "move on up a little higher!"—Bless God!

MAMA *(A little drily, doubting the total sincerity of the Blesser)* Bless God.

JOHNSON He's good, ain't He?

MAMA Oh yes, He's good.

JOHNSON I mean sometimes He works in mysterious ways . . . but He works, don't He!

MAMA *(The same)* Yes, he does.

JOHNSON I'm just sooooooo happy for y'all. And this here child—*(About* RUTH*)* looks like she could just pop open with happiness, don't she. Where's all the rest of the family?

MAMA Bennie's gone to bed—

JOHNSON Ain't no . . . (*The implication is pregnancy*) sickness done hit you—I hope . . . ?

MAMA No—she just tired. She was out this evening.

JOHNSON (*All is a coo, an empathetic coo*) Aw—ain't that lovely. She still going out with the little Murchison boy?

MAMA (*Drily*) Ummmm huh.

JOHNSON That's lovely. You sure got lovely children, Younger. Me and Isaiah talks all the time 'bout what fine children you was blessed with. We sure do.

MAMA Ruth, give Mis' Johnson a piece of sweet potato pie and some milk.

JOHNSON Oh honey, I can't stay hardly a minute—I just dropped in to see if there was anything I could do. (*Accepting the food easily*) I guess y'all seen the news what's all over the colored paper this week . . .

MAMA No—didn't get mine yet this week.

JOHNSON (*Lifting her head and blinking with the spirit of catastrophe*) You mean you ain't read 'bout them colored people that was bombed out their place out there?

(RUTH *straightens with concern and takes the paper and reads it.* JOHNSON *notices her face and feels commentary*)

JOHNSON Ain't it something how bad these here white folks is getting here in Chicago! Lord, getting so you think you right down in Mississippi! (*With a tremendous and rather insincere sense of melodrama*) 'Course I thinks it's wonderful how our folks keeps on pushing out. You hear some of these Negroes 'round here talking 'bout how they don't go where they ain't wanted and all that—but not me, honey! (*This is a lie*) Wilhemenia Othella Johnson goes anywhere, any time she feels like it! (*With head movement for emphasis*) Yes I do! Why if we left it up to these here crackers, the poor niggers wouldn't have nothing—(*She clasps her hand over her mouth*) Oh, I always forgets you don't 'low that word in your house.

MAMA (*Quietly, looking at her*) No—I don't 'low it.

JOHNSON (*Vigorously again*) Me neither! I was just telling Isaiah yesterday when he come using it in front of me—I said, "Isaiah, it's just like Mis' Younger says all the time—"

MAMA Don't you want some more pie?

JOHNSON No—no thank you; this was lovely. I got to get on over home and have my midnight coffee. I hear some people say it don't let them sleep but I finds I can't close my eyes right lessen I done had that laaaast cup of coffee . . . (*She waits. A beat. Undaunted*) My Goodnight coffee, I calls it!

MAMA (*With much eye-rolling and communication between herself and* RUTH) Ruth, why don't you give Mis' Johnson some coffee.

(RUTH *gives* MAMA *an unpleasant look for her kindness*)

JOHNSON (*Accepting the coffee*) Where's Brother tonight?

MAMA He's lying down.

JOHNSON Mmmmmm, he sure gets his beauty rest, don't he? Good-looking man. Sure is a good-looking man! (*Reaching out to pat* RUTH'S *stomach again*) I guess that's how come we keep having babies around here. (*She winks at* MAMA) One thing 'bout Brother, he always know how to have a *good* time. And soooooo ambitious! I bet it was his idea y'all moving out to Clybourne Park. Lord—I bet this time next month y'all's names will have been in the papers plenty—(*Holding up her hands to mark off each word of the headline she can see in front of her*) "NEGROES INVADE CLYBOURNE PARK—BOMBED!"

MAMA (*She and* RUTH *look at the woman in amazement*) We ain't exactly moving out there to get bombed.

JOHNSON Oh, honey—you know I'm praying to God every day that don't nothing like that happen! But you have to think of life like it is—and these here Chicago peckerwoods is some baaaad peckerwoods.

MAMA (*Wearily*) We done thought all about that Mis' Johnson.

(BENEATHA *comes out of the bedroom in her robe and passes through to the bathroom.* MRS. JOHNSON *turns*)

JOHNSON Hello there, Bennie!

BENEATHA (*Crisply*) Hello, Mrs. Johnson.

JOHNSON How is school?

BENEATHA (*Crisply*) Fine, thank you. (*She goes out.*)

JOHNSON (*Insulted*) Getting so she don't have much to say to nobody.

MAMA The child was on her way to the bathroom.

JOHNSON I know—but sometimes she act like ain't got time to pass the time of day with nobody ain't been to college. Oh—I ain't criticizing her none. It's just—you know how some of our young people gets when they get a little education. *(MAMA and RUTH say nothing, just look at her)* Yes—well. Well, I guess I better get on home. *(Unmoving)* 'Course I can understand how she must be proud and everything—being the only one in the family to make something of herself. I know just being a chauffeur ain't never satisfied Brother none. He shouldn't feel like that, though. Ain't nothing wrong with being a chauffeur.

MAMA There's plenty wrong with it.

JOHNSON What?

MAMA Plenty. My husband always said being any kind of a servant wasn't a fit thing for a man to have to be. He always said a man's hands was made to make things, or to turn the earth with—not to drive nobody's car for 'em—or—*(She looks at her own hands)* carry they slop jars. And my boy is just like him—he wasn't meant to wait on nobody.

JOHNSON *(Rising, somewhat offended)* Mmmmmmmmm. The Youngers is too much for me! *(She looks around)* You sure one proud-acting bunch of colored folks. Well—I always thinks like Booker T. Washington said that time—"Education has spoiled many a good plow hand"—

MAMA Is that what old Booker T. said?

JOHNSON He sure did.

MAMA Well, it sounds just like him. The fool.

JOHNSON *(Indignantly)* Well—he was one of our great men.

MAMA Who said so?

JOHNSON *(Nonplussed)* You know, me and you ain't never agreed about some things, Lena Younger. I guess I better be going—

RUTH *(Quickly)* Good night.

JOHNSON Good night. Oh—*(Thrusting it at her)* You can keep the paper! *(With a trill)* 'Night.

MAMA Good night, Mis' Johnson.

(MRS. JOHNSON exits)

RUTH If ignorance was gold . . .

MAMA Shush. Don't talk about folks behind their backs.

RUTH You do.

MAMA I'm old and corrupted. (BENEATHA *enters*) You was rude to Mis' Johnson, Beneatha, and I don't like it at all.

BENEATHA (*At the door*) Mama, if there are two things we, as people, have got to overcome, one is the Ku Klux Klan—and the other is Mrs. Johnson. (*She exits*)

MAMA Smart aleck.

(*The phone rings*)

RUTH I'll get it.

MAMA Lord, ain't this a popular place tonight.

RUTH (*At the phone*) Hello—Just a minute. (*Goes to door*) Walter, it's Mrs. Arnold. (*Waits. Goes back to the phone. Tense*) Hello. Yes, this is his wife speaking . . . He's lying down now. Yes . . . well, he'll be in tomorrow. He's been very sick. Yes—I know we should have called, but we were so sure he'd be able to come in today. Yes—yes, I'm very sorry. Yes . . . Thank you very much. (*She hangs up.* WALTER *is standing in the doorway of the bedroom behind her*) That was Mrs. Arnold.

WALTER (*Indifferently*) Was it?

RUTH She said if you don't come in tomorrow that they are getting a new man . . .

WALTER Ain't that sad—ain't that crying sad.

RUTH She said Mr. Arnold has had to take a cab for three days . . . Walter, you ain't been to work for three days! (*This is a revelation to her*) Where you been, Walter Lee Younger? (WALTER *looks at her and starts to laugh*) You're going to lose your job.

WALTER That's right . . . (*He turns on the radio*)

RUTH Oh, Walter, and with your mother working like a dog every day—

(*A steamy, deep blues pours into the room*)

WALTER That's sad too—Everything is sad.

MAMA What have you been doing for these three days, son?

WALTER Mama—you don't know all the things a man what got leisure can find to do in this city . . . What's this—Friday night? Well—Wednesday I borrowed Willy Harris' car and I went for a drive . . . just me and myself and I drove and drove . . . Way out . . . way past South Chicago, and I parked the car and I sat and looked at the steel mills all day long. I just sat in the car and looked at them big black chimneys for hours. Then I drove back and I went to the Green Hat. (*Pause*) And Thursday—Thursday I borrowed the car again and I got in it and I pointed it the other way and I drove the other way—for hours—way, way up to Wisconsin, and I looked at the farms. I just drove and looked at the farms. Then I drove back and I went to the Green Hat. (*Pause*) And today—today I didn't get the car. Today I just walked. All over the Southside. And I looked at the Negroes and they looked at me and finally I just sat down on the curb at Thirty-ninth and South Parkway and I just sat there and watched the Negroes go by. And then I went to the Green Hat. You all sad? You all depressed? And you know where I am going right now—

(RUTH *goes out quietly*)

MAMA Oh, Big Walter, is this the harvest of our days?

WALTER You know what I like about the Green Hat? I like this little cat they got there who blows a sax . . . He blows. He talks to me. He ain't but 'bout five feet tall and he's got a conked head and his eyes is always closed and he's all music—

MAMA (*Rising and getting some papers out of her handbag*) Walter—

WALTER And there's this other guy who plays the piano . . . and they got a sound. I mean they can work on some music . . . They got the best little combo in the world in the Green Hat . . . You can just sit there and drink and listen to them three men play and you realize that don't nothing matter worth a damn, but just being there—

MAMA I've helped do it to you, haven't I, son? Walter I been wrong.

WALTER Naw—you ain't never been wrong about nothing, Mama.

MAMA Listen to me. I say I been wrong, son. That I been doing to you what the rest of the world been doing to you. (*She turns off the radio*) Walter—(*She stops and he looks up slowly at her and she meets his eyes pleadingly*) What you ain't never understood is that I ain't got nothing, don't own nothing, ain't never really wanted nothing that wasn't for you. There ain't nothing as precious to me . . . There ain't nothing worth holding on to, money, dreams, nothing else—if it means—if it means it's going to destroy my boy. (*She takes an envelope out of her handbag and puts it in front of him and he watches her without speaking or moving*) I paid the man thirty-five hundred dollars down on the house. That leaves sixty-five hundred dollars. Monday morning I want you to take this money and take three thousand dollars and put it in a savings account for Beneatha's medical schooling. The rest you put in a checking account—with your name on it. And from now on any penny that come out of it or that go in it is for you to look after. For you to decide. (*She drops her hands a little helplessly*) It ain't much, but it's all I got in the world and I'm putting it in your hands. I'm telling you to be the head of this family from now on like you supposed to be.

WALTER (*Stares at the money*) You trust me like that, Mama?

MAMA I ain't never stop trusting you. Like I ain't never stop loving you.

(*She goes out, and* WALTER *sits looking at the money on the table. Finally, in a decisive gesture, he gets up, and, in mingled joy and desperation, picks up the money. At the same moment,* TRAVIS *enters for bed*)

TRAVIS What's the matter, Daddy? You drunk?

WALTER (*Sweetly, more sweetly than we have ever known him*) No, Daddy ain't drunk. Daddy ain't going to never be drunk again . . .

TRAVIS Well, good night, Daddy.

(*The* FATHER *has come from behind the couch and leans over, embracing his son*)

WALTER Son, I feel like talking to you tonight.

TRAVIS About what?

WALTER Oh, about a lot of things. About you and what kind of man you going to be when you grow up. . . . Son—son, what do you want to be when you grow up?

TRAVIS A bus driver.

WALTER (*Laughing a little*) A what? Man, that ain't nothing to want to be!

TRAVIS Why not?

WALTER 'Cause, man—it ain't big enough—you know what I mean.

TRAVIS I don't know then. I can't make up my mind. Sometimes Mama asks me that too. And sometimes when I tell her I just want to be like you—she says she don't want me to be like that and sometimes she says she does. . . .

WALTER (*Gathering him up in his arms*) You know what, Travis? In seven years you going to be seventeen years old. And things is going to be very different with us in seven years, Travis. . . . One day when you are seventeen I'll come home—home from my office downtown somewhere—

TRAVIS You don't work in no office, Daddy.

WALTER No—but after tonight. After what your daddy gonna do tonight, there's going to be offices—a whole lot of offices . . .

TRAVIS What you gonna do tonight, Daddy?

WALTER You wouldn't understand yet, son, but your daddy's gonna make a transaction . . . a business transaction that's going to change our lives. . . . That's how come one day when you 'bout seventeen years old I'll come home and I'll be pretty tired, you know what I mean, after a day of conferences and secretaries getting things wrong the way they do . . . 'cause an executive's life is hell, man—(*The more he talks the farther away he gets*) And I'll pull the car up on the driveway . . . just a plain black Chrysler, I think, with white walls—no—black tires. More elegant. Rich people don't have to be flashy . . . though I'll have to get something a little sportier for Ruth—maybe a Cadillac convertible to do her shopping in. . . . And I'll come up the steps to the house and the gardener will be clipping away at the hedges and he'll say, "Good evening, Mr. Younger." And I'll say, "Hello, Jefferson, how are you this evening?" And I'll go inside and Ruth will come downstairs and meet me at the door and we'll kiss each other and she'll take my arm and we'll go up to your room to see you sitting on the floor with the catalogues of all the great schools in America around you. . . . All the great schools in the world! And—and I'll say, all right son—it's your seventeenth birthday, what is it you've decided? . . . Just tell me where you want to go to school and you'll *go*. Just tell me, what it is you want to be—and you'll *be* it. . . . Whatever you want to be—Yessir! (*He holds his arms open for* TRAVIS) You just name it, son . . . (TRAVIS *leaps into them*) and I hand you the world!

(WALTER'S *voice has risen in pitch and hysterical promise and on the last line he lifts* TRAVIS *high*)

Blackout

SCENE THREE

Time: Saturday, moving day, one week later.

Before the curtain rises, RUTH'S *voice, a strident, dramatic church alto, cuts through the silence.*

It is, in the darkness, a triumphant surge, a penetrating statement of expectation: "Oh, Lord, I don't feel no ways tired! Children, oh, glory hallelujah!"

As the curtain rises we see that RUTH *is alone in the living room, finishing up the family's packing. It is moving day. She is nailing crates and tying cartons.* BENEATHA *enters, carrying a guitar case, and watches her exuberant sister-in-law.*

RUTH Hey!

BENEATHA *(Putting away the case)* Hi.

RUTH *(Pointing at a package)* Honey—look in that package there and see what I found on sale this morning at the South Center. (RUTH *gets up and moves to the package and draws out some curtains)* Lookahere—hand-turned hems!

BENEATHA How do you know the window size out there?

RUTH *(Who hadn't thought of that)* Oh—Well, they bound to fit something in the whole house. Anyhow, they was too good a bargain to pass up. (RUTH *slaps her head, suddenly remembering something)* Oh, Bennie—I meant to put a special note on that carton over there. That's your mama's good china and she wants 'em to be very careful with it.

BENEATHA I'll do it.

*(*BENEATHA *finds a piece of paper and starts to draw large letters on it)*

RUTH You know what I'm going to do soon as I get in that new house?

BENEATHA What?

RUTH Honey—I'm going to run me a tub of water up to here . . . *(With her fingers practically up to her nostrils)* And I'm going to get in it—and I am going to sit . . . and sit . . . and sit in that hot water and the first person who knocks to tell me to hurry up and come out—

BENEATHA Gets shot at sunrise.

RUTH *(Laughing happily)* You said it, sister! *(Noticing how large* BENEATHA *is absent-mindedly making the note)* Honey, they ain't going to read that from no airplane.

BENEATHA (*Laughing herself*) I guess I always think things have more emphasis if they are big, somehow.

RUTH (*Looking up at her and smiling*) You and your brother seem to have that as a philosophy of life. Lord, that man—done changed so 'round here. You know—you know what we did last night? Me and Walter Lee?

BENEATHA What?

RUTH (*Smiling to herself*) We went to the movies. (*Looking at* BENEATHA *to see if she understands*) We went to the movies. You know the last time me and Walter went to the movies together?

BENEATHA No.

RUTH Me neither. That's how long it been. (*Smiling again*) But we went last night. The picture wasn't much good, but that didn't seem to matter. We went—and we held hands.

BENEATHA Oh, Lord!

RUTH We held hands—and you know what?

BENEATHA What?

RUTH When we come out of the show it was late and dark and all the stores and things was closed up . . . and it was kind of chilly and there wasn't many people on the streets . . . and we was still holding hands, me and Walter.

BENEATHA You're killing me.

(WALTER *enters with a large package. His happiness is deep in him; he cannot keep still with his newfound exuberance. He is singing and wiggling and snapping his fingers. He puts his package in a corner and puts a phonograph record, which he has brought in with him, on the record player. As the music, soulful and sensuous, comes up he dances over to* RUTH *and tries to get her to dance with him. She gives in at last to his raunchiness and in a fit of giggling allows herself to be drawn into his mood. They dip and she melts into his arms in a classic, body-melding "slow drag"*)

BENEATHA (*Regarding them a long time as they dance, then drawing in her breath for a deeply exaggerated comment which she does not particularly mean*) Talk about—olddddddddddd-fashionedddddddd—Negroes!

WALTER (*Stopping momentarily*) What kind of Negroes? (*He says this in fun. He is not angry with her today, nor with anyone. He starts to dance with his wife again*)

BENEATHA Old-fashioned.

WALTER (*As he dances with* RUTH) You know, when these New Negroes have their convention—(*Pointing at his sister*)—that is going to be the chairman of the Committee on Unending Agitation. (*He goes on dancing, then stops*) Race, race, race! . . . Girl, I do believe you are the first person in the history of the entire human race to successfully brainwash yourself. (BENEATHA *breaks up and he goes on dancing. He stops again, enjoying his tease*) Damn, even the N double A C P takes a holiday sometimes! (BENEATHA *and* RUTH *laugh. He dances with* RUTH *some more and starts to laugh and stops and pantomimes someone over an operating table*) I can just see that chick someday looking down at some poor cat on an operating table and before she starts to slice him, she says . . . (*Pulling his sleeves back maliciously*) "By the way, what are your views on civil rights down there? . . ."

(*He laughs at her again and starts to dance happily. The bell sounds*)

BENEATHA Sticks and stones may break my bones but . . . words will never hurt me!

(BENEATHA *goes to the door and opens it as* WALTER *and* RUTH *go on with the clowning.* BENEATHA *is somewhat surprised to see a quiet-looking middle-aged white man in a business suit holding his hat and a briefcase in his hand and consulting a small piece of paper*)

MAN Uh—how do you do, miss. I am looking for a Mrs.—(*He looks at the slip of paper*) Mrs. Lena Younger? (*He stops short, struck dumb at the sight of the oblivious* WALTER *and* RUTH)

BENEATHA (*Smoothing her hair with slight embarrassment*) Oh—yes, that's my mother. Excuse me (*She closes the door and turns to quiet the other two*) Ruth! Brother! (*Enunciating precisely but soundlessly: "There's a white man at the door!" They stop dancing,* RUTH *cuts off the phonograph,* BENEATHA *opens the door. The man casts a curious quick glance at all of them*) Uh—come in please.

MAN (*Coming in*) Thank you.

BENEATHA My mother isn't here just now. Is it business?

MAN Yes . . . well, of a sort.

WALTER (*Freely, the Man of the House*) Have a seat. I'm Mrs. Younger's son. I look after most of her business matters.

(RUTH *and* BENEATHA *exchange amused glances*)

MAN (*Regarding* WALTER, *and sitting*) Well—My name is Karl Lindner . . .

WALTER (*Stretching out his hand*) Walter Younger. This is my wife—(RUTH *nods politely*)—and my sister.

LINDNER How do you do.

WALTER (*Amiably, as he sits himself easily on a chair, leaning forward on his knees with interest and looking expectantly into the newcomer's face*) What can we do for you, Mr. Lindner!

LINDNER (*Some minor shuffling of the hat and briefcase on his knees*) Well—I am a representative of the Clybourne Park Improvement Association—

WALTER (*Pointing*) Why don't you sit your things on the floor?

LINDNER Oh—yes. Thank you. (*He slides the briefcase and hat under the chair*) And as I was saying—I am from the Clybourne Park Improvement Association and we have had it brought to our attention at the last meeting that you people—or at least your mother—has bought a piece of residential property at—(*He digs for the slip of paper again*)—four o six Clybourne Street . . .

WALTER That's right. Care for something to drink? Ruth, get Mr. Lindner a beer.

LINDNER (*Upset for some reason*) Oh—no, really. I mean thank you very much, but no thank you.

RUTH (*Innocently*) Some coffee?

LINDNER Thank you, nothing at all.

(BENEATHA *is watching the man carefully*)

LINDNER Well, I don't know how much you folks know about our organization. (*He is a gentle man; thoughtful and somewhat labored in his manner*) It is one of these community organizations set up to look after—oh, you know, things like block upkeep and special projects and we also have what we call our New Neighbors Orientation Committee . . .

BENEATHA (*Drily*) Yes—and what do they do?

LINDNER (*Turning a little to her and then returning the main force to* WALTER) Well—it's what you might call a sort of welcoming committee, I guess. I mean they, we—I'm chairman of the committee—go around and see the new people who move into the neighborhood and sort of give them the lowdown on the way we do things out in Clybourne Park.

BENEATHA (*With appreciation of the two meanings, which escape* RUTH *and* WALTER) Un-huh.

LINDNER And we also have the category of what the association calls—(*He looks elsewhere*)—uh—special community problems . . .

BENEATHA Yes—and what are some of those?

WALTER Girl, let the man talk.

LINDNER (*With understated relief*) Thank you. I would sort of like to explain this thing in my own way. I mean I want to explain to you in a certain way.

WALTER Go ahead.

LINDNER Yes. Well. I'm going to try to get right to the point. I'm sure we'll all appreciate that in the long run.

BENEATHA Yes.

WALTER Be still now!

LINDNER Well—

RUTH (*Still innocently*) Would you like another chair—you don't look comfortable.

LINDNER (*More frustrated than annoyed*) No, thank you very much. Please. Well—to get right to the point I—(*A great breath, and he is off at last*) I am sure you people must be aware of some of the incidents which have happened in various parts of the city when colored people have moved into certain areas—(BENEATHA *exhales heavily and starts tossing a piece of fruit up and down in the air*) Well—because we have what I think is going to be a unique type of organization in American community life—not only do we deplore that kind of thing—but we are trying to do something about it. (BENEATHA *stops tossing and turns with a new and quizzical interest to the man*) We feel—(*gaining confidence in his mission because of the interest in the faces of the people he is talking to*)—we feel that most of the trouble in this world, when you come right down to it—(*He hits his knee for emphasis*)—most of the trouble exists because people just don't sit down and talk to each other.

RUTH (*Nodding as she might in church, pleased with the remark*) You can say that again, mister.

LINDNER (*More encouraged by such affirmation*) That we don't try hard enough in this world to understand the other fellow's problem. The other guy's point of view.

RUTH Now that's right.

(BENEATHA *and* WALTER *merely watch and listen with genuine interest*)

LINDNER Yes—that's the way we feel out in Clybourne Park. And that's why I was elected to come here this afternoon and talk to you people. Friendly like, you know, the way people should talk to each other and see if we couldn't find some way to work this thing out. As I say, the whole business is a matter of *caring* about the other fellow. Anybody can see that you are a nice family of folks, hard working and honest I'm sure. (BENEATHA *frowns slightly, quizzically, her head tilted regarding him*) Today everybody knows what it means to be on the outside of *something*. And of course, there is always somebody who is out to take advantage of some people who don't always understand.

WALTER What do you mean?

LINDNER Well—you see our community is made up of people who've worked hard as the dickens for years to build up that little community. They're not rich and fancy people; just hard-working, honest people who don't really have much but those little homes and a dream of the kind of community they want to raise their children in. Now, I don't say we are perfect and there is a lot wrong in some of the things they want. But you've got to admit that a man, right or wrong, has the right to want to have the neighborhood he lives in a certain kind of way. And at the moment the overwhelming majority of our people out there feel that people get along better, take more of a common interest in the life of the community, when they share a common background. I want you to believe me when I tell you that race prejudice simply doesn't enter into it. It is a matter of the people of Clybourne Park believing, rightly or wrongly, as I say, that for the happiness of all concerned that our Negro families are happier when they live in their *own* communities.

BENEATHA (*With a grand and bitter gesture*) This, friends, is the Welcoming Committee!

WALTER (*Dumbfounded, looking at* LINDNER) Is this what you came marching all the way over here to tell us?

LINDNER Well, now we've been having a fine conversation. I hope you'll hear me all the way through.

WALTER *(Tightly)* Go ahead, man.

LINDNER You see—in the face of all the things I have said, we are prepared to make your family a very generous offer . . .

BENEATHA Thirty pieces and not a coin less!

WALTER Yeah?

LINDNER *(Putting on his glasses and drawing a form out of the briefcase)* Our association is prepared, through the collective effort of our people, to buy the house from you at a financial gain to your family.

RUTH Lord have mercy, ain't this the living gall!

WALTER All right, you through?

LINDNER Well, I want to give you the exact terms of the financial arrangement—

WALTER We don't want to hear no exact terms of no arrangements. I want to know if you got any more to tell us 'bout getting together?

LINDNER *(Taking off his glasses)* Well—I don't suppose that you feel . . .

WALTER Never mind how I feel—you got any more to say 'bout how people ought to sit down and talk to each other? . . . Get out of my house, man.

(He turns his back and walks to the door)

LINDNER *(Looking around at the hostile faces and reaching and assembling his hat and briefcase)* Well—I don't understand why you people are reacting this way. What do you think you are going to gain by moving into a neighborhood where you just aren't wanted and where some elements—well—people can get awful worked up when they feel that their whole way of life and everything they've ever worked for is threatened.

WALTER Get out.

LINDNER *(At the door, holding a small card)* Well—I'm sorry it went like this.

WALTER Get out.

LINDNER *(Almost sadly regarding WALTER)* You just can't force people to change their hearts, son.

(He turns and put his card on a table and exits. WALTER pushes the door to with stinging hatred, and stands looking at it. RUTH just sits and BENEATHA just stands. They say nothing. MAMA and TRAVIS enter)

MAMA   Well—this all the packing got done since I left out of here this morning. I testify before God that my children got all the energy of the *dead*! What time the moving men due?

BENEATHA   Four o'clock. You had a caller, Mama.
(*She is smiling, teasingly*)

MAMA   Sure enough—who?

BENEATHA   (*Her arms folded saucily*) The Welcoming Committee.

(WALTER *and* RUTH *giggle*)

MAMA   (*Innocently*) Who?

BENEATHA   The Welcoming Committee. They said they're sure going to be glad to see you when you get there.

WALTER   (*Devilishly*) Yeah, they said they can't hardly wait to see your face.
(*Laughter*)

MAMA   (*Sensing their facetiousness*) What's the matter with you all?

WALTER   Ain't nothing the matter with us. We just telling you 'bout the gentleman who came to see you this afternoon. From the Clybourne Park Improvement Association.

MAMA   What he want?

RUTH   (*In the same mood as* BENEATHA *and* WALTER) To welcome you, honey.

WALTER   He said they can't hardly wait. He said the one thing they don't have, that they just *dying* to have out there is a fine family of fine colored people! (*To* RUTH *and* BENEATHA) Ain't that right!

RUTH   (*Mockingly*) Yeah! He left his card—

BENEATHA   (*Handing card to* MAMA) In case.

(MAMA *reads and throws it on the floor—understanding and looking off as she draws her chair up to the table on which she has put her plant and some sticks and some cord*)

MAMA   Father, give us strength. (*Knowingly—and without fun*) Did he threaten us?

BENEATHA   Oh—Mama—they don't do it like that any more. He talked Brotherhood. He said everybody ought to learn how to sit down and hate each other with good Christian fellowship.

(*She and* WALTER *shake hands to ridicule the remark*)

MAMA *(Sadly)* Lord, protect us . . .

RUTH You should hear the money those folks raised to buy the house from us. All we paid and then some.

BENEATHA What they think we going to do—eat 'em?

RUTH No, honey, marry 'em.

MAMA *(Shaking her head)* Lord, Lord, Lord . . .

RUTH Well—that's the way the crackers crumble. *(A beat)* Joke.

BENEATHA *(Laughingly noticing what her mother is doing)* Mama, what are you doing?

MAMA Fixing my plant so it won't get hurt none on the way . . .

BENEATHA Mama, you going to take *that* to the new house?

MAMA Un-huh—

BENEATHA That raggedy-looking old thing?

MAMA *(Stopping and looked at her)* It expresses ME!

RUTH *(With delight, to* BENEATHA*)* So there, Miss Thing!

(WALTER comes to MAMA suddenly and bends down behind her and squeezes her in his arms with all his strength. She is overwhelmed by the suddenness of it and, though delighted, her manner is like that of RUTH and TRAVIS)

MAMA Look out now, boy! You make me mess up my thing here!

WALTER *(His face lit, he slips down on his knees beside her, his arms still about her)* Mama . . . you know what it means to climb up in the chariot?

MAMA *(Gruffly, very happy)* Get on away from me now . . .

RUTH *(Near the gift-wrapped package, trying to catch* WALTER'S *eye)* Psst—

WALTER What the old song say, Mama . . .

RUTH Walter—Now?

(She is pointing at the package)

WALTER *(Speaking the lines, sweetly, playfully, in his mother's face)*
I got wings . . . you got wings . . .
All God's children got wings . . .

MAMA Boy—get out of my face and do some work . . .

WALTER.
> When I get to heaven gonna put on my wings,
> Gonna fly all over God's heaven . . .

BENEATHA *(Teasingly, from across the room)* Everybody talking 'bout heaven ain't going there!

WALTER *(To* RUTH, *who is carrying the box across to them)* I don't know, you think we ought to give her that . . . Seems to me she ain't been very appreciative around here.

MAMA *(Eyeing the box, which is obviously a gift)* What is that?

WALTER *(Taking it from* RUTH *and putting it on the table in front of* MAMA) Well—what you all think? Should we give it to her?

RUTH Oh—she was pretty good today.

MAMA I'll good you—

(She turns her eyes to the box again)

BENEATHA Open it, Mama.

(She stands up, looks at it, turns and looks at all of them, and then presses her hands together and does not open the package)

WALTER *(Sweetly)* Open it, Mama. It's for you. (MAMA *looks in his eyes. It is the first present in her life without its being Christmas. Slowly she opens her package and lifts out, one by one, a brand-new sparkling set of gardening tools.* WALTER *continues, prodding)* Ruth made up the note—read it . . .

MAMA *(Picking up the card and adjusting her glasses)* "To our own Mrs. Miniver—Love from Brother, Ruth and Beneatha." Ain't that lovely . . .

TRAVIS *(Tugging at his father's sleeve)* Daddy, can I give her mine now?

WALTER All right, son. (TRAVIS *flies to get his gift)*

MAMA Now I don't have to use my knives and forks no more . . .

WALTER Travis didn't want to go in with the rest of us, Mama. He got his own. *(Somewhat amused)* We don't know what it is . . .

TRAVIS *(Racing back in the room with a large hatbox and putting it in front of his grandmother)* Here!

MAMA Lord have mercy, baby. You done gone and bought your grandmother a hat?

TRAVIS (*Very proud*) Open it!

(*She does and lifts out an elaborate, but very elaborate, wide gardening hat, and all the adults break up at the sight of it.*)

RUTH Travis, honey, what is that?

TRAVIS (*Who thinks it is beautiful and appropriate*) It's a gardening hat! Like the ladies always have on in the magazines when they work in their gardens.

BENEATHA (*Giggling fiercely*) Travis—we were trying to make Mama Mrs. Miniver—not Scarlett O'Hara!

MAMA (*Indignantly*) What's the matter with you all! This here is a beautiful hat! (*Absurdly*) I always wanted me one just like it!

(*She pops it on her head to prove it to her grandson, and the hat is ludicrous and considerably oversized*)

RUTH Hot dog! Go, Mama!

WALTER (*Doubled over with laughter*) I'm sorry, Mama—but you look like you ready to go out and chop you some cotton sure enough!

(*They all laugh except* MAMA, *out of deference to* TRAVIS' *feelings*)

MAMA (*Gathering the boy up to her*) Bless your heart—this is the prettiest hat I ever owned—(WALTER, RUTH and BENEATHA *chime in—noisily, festively and insincerely congratulating* TRAVIS *on his gift*) What are we all standing around here for? We ain't finished packin' yet. Bennie, you ain't packed one book.

(*The bell rings*)

BENEATHA That couldn't be the movers . . . it's not hardly two good yet—

(BENEATHA *goes into her room.* MAMA *starts for door*)

WALTER (*Turning, stiffening*) Wait—wait—I'll get it.

(*He stands and looks at the door*)

MAMA You expecting company, son?

WALTER (*Just looking at the door*) Yeah—yeah . . .

(MAMA *looks at* RUTH, *and they exchange innocent and unfrightened glances*)

MAMA (*Not understanding*) Well, let them in, son.

BENEATHA (*From her room*) We need some more string.

MAMA   Travis—you run to the hardware and get me some string cord.

(MAMA *goes out and* WALTER *turns and looks at* RUTH. TRAVIS *goes to a dish for money*)

RUTH   Why don't you answer the door, man?

WALTER   (*Suddenly bounding across the floor to embrace her*) 'Cause sometimes it hard to let the future begin! (*Stooping down in her face*)
I got wings! You got wings!
All God's children got wings!

(*He crosses to the door and throws it open. Standing there is a very slight little man in a not too prosperous business suit and with haunted frightened eyes and a hat pulled down tightly, brim up, around his forehead.* TRAVIS *passes between the men and exits.* WALTER *leans deep in the man's face, still in his jubilance*)

When I get to heaven gonna put on my wings,
Gonna fly all over God's heaven . . .

(*The little man just stares at him*)

Heaven—

(*Suddenly he stops and looks past the little man into the empty hallway*)
Where's Willy, man?

BOBO   He ain't with me.

WALTER   (*Not disturbed*) Oh—come on in. You know my wife.

BOBO   (*Dumbly, taking off his hat*) Yes—h'you, Miss Ruth?

RUTH   (*Quietly, a mood apart from her husband already, seeing* BOBO) Hello, Bobo.

WALTER   You right on time today . . . Right on time. That's the way! (*He slaps* BOBO *on his back*) Sit down . . . lemme hear.

(RUTH *stands stiffly and quietly in back of them, as though somehow she senses death, her eyes fixed on her husband*)

BOBO   (*His frightened eyes on the floor, his hat in his hands*) Could I please get a drink of water, before I tell you about it, Walter Lee?

(WALTER *does not take his eyes off the man.* RUTH *goes blindly to the tap and gets a glass of water and brings it to* BOBO)

WALTER   There ain't nothing wrong, is there?

BOBO Lemme tell you—

WALTER Man—didn't nothing go wrong?

BOBO Lemme tell you—Walter Lee. (*Looking at* RUTH *and talking to her more than to* WALTER) You know how it was. I got to tell you how it was. I mean first I got to tell you how it was all the way . . . I mean about the money I put in, Walter Lee . . .

WALTER (*With taut agitation now*) What about the money you put in?

BOBO Well—it wasn't much as we told you—me and Willy—(*He stops*) I'm sorry, Walter. I got a bad feeling about it. I got a real bad feeling about it . . .

WALTER Man, what you telling me about all this for? . . . Tell me what happened in Springfield . . .

BOBO Springfield.

RUTH (*Like a dead woman*) What was supposed to happen in Springfield?

BOBO (*To her*) This deal that me and Walter went into with Willy— Me and Willy was going to go down to Springfield and spread some money 'round so's we wouldn't have to wait so long for the liquor license . . . That's what we were going to do. Everybody said that was the way you had to do, you understand, Miss Ruth?

WALTER Man—what happened down there?

BOBO (*A pitiful man, near tears*) I'm trying to tell you, Walter.

WALTER (*Screaming at him suddenly*) THEN TELL ME, GODDAMMIT . . . WHAT'S THE MATTER WITH YOU?

BOBO Man . . . I didn't go to no Springfield, yesterday.

WALTER (*Halted, life hanging in the moment*) Why not?

BOBO (*The long way, the hard way to tell*) 'Cause I didn't have no reasons to . . .

WALTER Man, what are you talking about!

BOBO I'm talking about the fact that when I got to the train station yesterday morning—eight o'clock like we planned . . . Man—*Willy didn't never show up*.

WALTER Why . . . where was he . . . where is he?

BOBO That's what I'm trying to tell you. I don't know . . . I waited six hours . . . I called his house . . . and I waited . . . six hours . . . I waited in that train station six hours . . . (*Breaking into tears*) That was all the extra money I had in the world . . . (*Looking up at* WALTER *with the tears running down his face*) Man, *Willy is gone*.

WALTER Gone, what you mean Willy is gone? Gone where? You mean he went by himself. You mean he went off to Springfield by himself—to take care of getting the license—(*Turns and looks anxiously at* RUTH) You mean maybe he didn't want too many people in on the business down there? (*Looks to* RUTH *again, as before*) You know Willy got his own ways. (*Looks back to* BOBO) Maybe you was late yesterday and he just went on down there without you. Maybe—maybe—he's been callin' you at home tryin' to tell you what happened or something. Maybe—maybe—he just got sick. He's somewhere—he's got to be somewhere. We just got to find him—me and you got to find him. (*Grabs* BOBO *senselessly by the collar and starts to shake him*) We got to!

BOBO (*In sudden angry, frightened agony*) What's the matter with you, Walter! *When a cat take off with your money he don't leave you no road maps!*

WALTER (*Turning madly, as though he is looking for* WILLY *in the very room*) Willy! . . . Willy . . . don't do it . . . Please don't do it . . . Man, not with that money . . . Man, please, not with that money . . . Oh, God . . . Don't let it be true . . . (*He is wandering around, crying out for* WILLY *and looking for him or perhaps for help from God*) Man . . . I trusted you . . . Man, I put my life in your hands . . . (*He starts to crumple down on the floor as* RUTH *just covers her face in horror.* MAMA *opens the door and comes into the room, with* BENEATHA *behind her*) Man . . . (*He starts to pound the floor with his fists, sobbing wildly*) THAT MONEY IS MADE OUT OF MY FATHER'S FLESH—

BOBO (*Standing over him helplessly*) I'm sorry, Walter . . . (*Only* WALTER'S *sobs reply.* BOBO *puts on his hat*) I had my life staked on this deal, too . . .

(*He exits*)

MAMA (*To* WALTER) Son—(*She goes to him, bends down to him, talks to his bent head*) Son . . . Is it gone? Son, I gave you sixty-five hundred dollars. Is it gone? All of it? Beneatha's money too?

WALTER (*Lifting his head slowly*) Mama . . . I never . . . went to the bank at all . . .

MAMA (*Not wanting to believe him*) You mean . . . your sister's school money . . . you used that too . . . Walter? . . .

WALTER Yessss! All of it . . . It's all gone . . .

(*There is total silence.* RUTH *stands with her face covered with her hands;* BENEATHA *leans forlornly against a wall, fingering a piece of red ribbon from the mother's gift.* MAMA *stops and looks at her son without recognition and then, quite without thinking about it, starts to beat him senselessly in the face.* BENEATHA *goes to them and stops it*)

BENEATHA Mama!

(MAMA *stops and looks at both of her children and rises slowly and wanders vaguely, aimlessly away from them*)

MAMA I seen . . . him . . . night after night . . . come in . . . and look at that rug . . . and then look at me . . . the red showing in his eyes . . . the veins moving in his head . . . I seen him grow thin and old before he was forty . . . working and working and working like somebody's old horse . . . killing himself . . . and you—you give it all away in a day —(*She raises her arms to strike him again*)

BENEATHA Mama—

MAMA Oh God . . . (*She looks up to Him*) Look down here—and show me the strength.

BENEATHA Mama—

MAMA (*Folding over*) Strength . . .

BENEATHA (*Plaintively*) Mama . . .

MAMA Strength!

Curtain

Act III

An hour later.

At curtain, there is a sullen light of gloom in the living room, gray light not unlike that which began the first scene of Act One. At left we can see WALTER *within his room alone with himself. He is stretched out on the bed, his shirt out and open, his arms under his head. He does not smoke, he does not cry out, he merely lies there, looking up at the ceiling, much as if he were alone in the world.*

In the living room BENEATHA *sits at the table, still surrounded by the now almost ominous packing crates. She sits looking off. We feel that this is a mood struck perhaps an hour before, and it lingers now, full of the empty sound of profound disappointment. We see on a line from her brother's bedroom the sameness of their attitudes. Presently the bell rings and* BENEATHA *rises without ambition or interest in answering. It is* ASAGAI, *smiling broadly, striding into the room with energy and happy expectation and conversation.*

ASAGAI   I came over . . . I had some free time. I thought I might help with the packing, Ah, I like the look of packing crates! A household in preparation for a journey! It depresses some people . . . but for me . . . it is another feeling. Something full of the flow of life, do you understand? Movement, progress . . . It makes me think of Africa.

BENEATHA   Africa!

ASAGAI   What kind of mood is this? Have I told you how deeply you move me?

BENEATHA   He gave away the money, Asagai . . .

ASAGAI   Who gave away what money?

BENEATHA   The insurance money. My brother gave it away.

ASAGAI   Gave it away?

BENEATHA   He made an investment! With a man even Travis wouldn't have trusted with his most worn-out marbles.

ASAGAI   And it's gone?

BENEATHA   Gone!

ASAGAI   I'm very sorry . . . And you, now?

BENEATHA Me? . . . Me? . . . Me, I'm nothing . . . Me. When I was very small . . . we used to take our sleds out in the wintertime and the only hills we had were the ice-covered stone steps of some houses down the street. And we used to fill them in with snow and make them smooth and slide down them all day . . . and it was very dangerous, you know . . . far too steep . . . and sure enough one day a kid named Rufus came down too fast and hit the sidewalk and we saw his face just split open right there in front of us . . . And I remember standing then looking at his bloody open face thinking that was the end of Rufus. But the ambulance came and they took him to the hospital and they fixed the broken bones and they sewed it all up . . . and the next time I saw Rufus he just had a little line down the middle of his face . . . I never got over that . . .

ASAGAI What?

BENEATHA That that was what one person could do for another, fix him up—sew up the problem, make him all right again. That was the most marvelous thing in the world . . . I wanted to do that. I always thought it was the one concrete thing in the world that a human being could do. Fix up the sick, you know—and make them whole again. This was truly being God . . .

ASAGAI You wanted to be God?

BENEATHA No—I wanted to cure. It used to be so important to me. I wanted to cure. It used to matter. I used to care. I mean about people and how their bodies hurt . . .

ASAGAI And you've stopped caring?

BENEATHA Yes—I think so.

ASAGAI Why?

BENEATHA (Bitterly) Because it doesn't seem deep enough, close enough to what ails mankind! It was a child's way of seeing things—or an idealist's.

ASAGAI Children see things very well sometimes—and idealists even better.

BENEATHA I know that's what you think. Because you are still where I left off. You with all your talk and dreams about Africa! You still think you can patch up the world. Cure the Great Sore of Colonialism—(Loftily, mocking it) with the Penicillin of Independence—!

ASAGAI Yes!

BENEATHA Independence *and then what?* What about all the crooks and thieves and just plain idiots who will come into power and steal and plunder the same as before—only now they will be black and do it in the name of the new Independence—WHAT ABOUT THEM?!

ASAGAI That will be the problem for another time. First we must get there.

BENEATHA And where does it end?

ASAGAI End? Who even spoke of an end? To life? To living?

BENEATHA An end to misery! To stupidity! Don't you see there isn't any real progress, Asagai, there is only one large circle that we march in, around and around, each of us with our own little picture in front of us—our own little mirage that we think is the future.

ASAGAI That is the mistake.

BENEATHA What?

ASAGAI What you just said about the circle. It isn't a circle—it is simply a long line—as in geometry, you know, one that reaches into infinity. And because we cannot see the end—we also cannot see how it changes. And it is very odd but those who see the changes—who dream, who will not give up—are called idealists . . . and those who see only the circle we call *them* the "realists"!

BENEATHA Asagai, while I was sleeping in that bed in there, people went out and took the future right out of my hands! And nobody asked me, nobody consulted me—they just went out and changed my life!

ASAGAI Was it your money?

BENEATHA What?

ASAGAI Was it your money he gave away?

BENEATHA It belonged to all of us.

ASAGAI But did you earn it? Would you have had it at all if your father had not died?

BENEATHA No.

ASAGAI Then isn't there something wrong in a house—in a world—where all dreams, good or bad, must depend on the death of a man? I never thought to see *you* like this, Alaiyo. You! Your brother made a mistake and you are grateful to him so that now you can give up the ailing human race on account of it! You talk about what good is struggle, what good is anything! Where are we all going and why are we bothering!

BENEATHA AND YOU CANNOT ANSWER IT!

ASAGAI (*Shouting over her*) *I LIVE THE ANSWER!* (*Pause*) In my village at home it is the exceptional man who can even read a newspaper . . . or who ever sees a book at all. I will go home and much of what I will have to say will seem strange to the people of my village. But I will teach and work and things will happen, slowly and swiftly. At times it will seem that nothing changes at all . . . and then again the sudden dramatic events which make history leap into the future. And then quiet again. Retrogression even. Guns, murder, revolution. And I even will have moments when I wonder if the quiet was not better than all that death and hatred. But I will look about my village at the illiteracy and disease and ignorance and I will not wonder long. And perhaps . . . perhaps I will be a great man . . . I mean perhaps I will hold on to the substance of truth and find my way always with the right course . . . and perhaps for it I will be butchered in my bed some night by the servants of empire . . .

BENEATHA *The martyr!*

ASAGAI (*He smiles*) . . . or perhaps I shall live to be a very old man, respected and esteemed in my new nation . . . And perhaps I shall hold office and this is what I'm trying to tell you, Alaiyo: Perhaps the things I believe now for my country will be wrong and outmoded, and I will not understand and do terrible things to have things my way or merely to keep my power. Don't you see that there will be young men and women—not British soldiers then, but my own black countrymen—to step out of the shadows some evening and slit my then useless throat? Don't you see they have always been there . . . that they always will be. And that such a thing as my own death will be an advance? They who might kill me even . . . actually replenish all that I was.

BENEATHA Oh, Asagai, I know all that.

ASAGAI Good! Then stop moaning and groaning and tell me what you plan to do.

BENEATHA Do?

ASAGAI I have a bit of a suggestion.

BENEATHA What?

ASAGAI (*Rather quietly for him*) That when it is all over—that you come home with me—

BENEATHA (*Staring at him and crossing away with exasperation*) Oh—Asagai—at this moment you decide to be romantic!

ASAGAI (*Quickly understanding the misunderstanding*) My dear, young creature of the New World—I do not mean across the city—I mean across the ocean: home—to Africa.

BENEATHA (*Slowly understanding and turning to him with murmured amazement*) To Africa?

ASAGAI Yes! . . . (*Smiling and lifting his arms playfully*) Three hundred years later the African Prince rose up out of the seas and swept the maiden back across the middle passage over which her ancestors had come—

BENEATHA (*Unable to play*) To—to Nigeria?

ASAGAI Nigeria. Home. (*Coming to her with genuine romantic flippancy*) I will show you our mountains and our stars; and give you cool drinks from gourds and teach you the old songs and the ways of our people—and, in time, we will pretend that—(*Very softly*)—you have only been away for a day. Say that you'll come (*He swings her around and takes her full in his arms in a kiss which proceeds to passion*)

BENEATHA (*Pulling away suddenly*) You're getting me all mixed up—

ASAGAI Why?

BENEATHA Too many things—too many things have happened today. I must sit down and think. I don't know what I feel about anything right this minute.

(*She promptly sits down and props her chin on her fist*)

ASAGAI (*Charmed*) All right, I shall leave you. No—don't get up. (*Touching her, gently, sweetly*) Just sit awhile and think . . . Never be afraid to sit awhile and think. (*He goes to door and looks at her*) How often I have looked at you and said, "Ah—so this is what the New World hath finally wrought . . ."

(*He exits.* BENEATHA *sits alone. Presently* WALTER *enters from his room and starts to rumble through things, feverishly looking for something. She looks up and turns in her seat*)

BENEATHA (*Hissingly*) Yes—just look at what the New World hath wrought! . . . Just look! (*She gestures with bitter disgust*) There he is! *Monsieur le petit bourgeois noir*—himself! There he is—Symbol of a Rising Class! Entrepreneur! Titan of the system! (WALTER *ignores her completely and continues frantically and destructively looking for something* and hurling things to floor and tearing things out of their place in his search. BENEATHA *ignores the eccentricity of his actions and goes on with the mono- logue of insult*) Did you dream of yachts on Lake Michigan, Brother? Did you see yourself on that Great Day sitting down at the Conference Table, surrounded by all the mighty bald-headed men in America? All halted, waiting, breathless, waiting for your pronouncements on industry? Waiting for you—Chairman of the Board! (WALTER *finds what he is looking for—a small piece of white paper—and pushes it in his pocket and puts on his coat and rushes out without ever having looked at her. She shouts after him*) I look around at you and I see the final triumph of stupidity in the world!

(*The door slams and she returns to just sitting again.* RUTH *comes quickly out of* MAMA'S *room*)

RUTH Who was that?

BENEATHA Your husband.

RUTH Where did he go?

BENEATHA Who knows—maybe he has an appointment at U.S. Steel.

RUTH (*Anxiously, with frightened eyes*) You didn't say nothing bad to him, did you?

BENEATHA Bad? Say anything bad to him? No—I told him he was a sweet boy and full of dreams and everything is strictly peachy keen, as the ofay kids say!

(MAMA *enters from her bedroom. She is lost, vague, trying to catch hold, to make some sense of her former command of the world, but it still eludes her. A sense of waste overwhelms her gait; a measure of apology rides on her shoulders. She goes to her plant, which has remained on the table, looks at it, picks it up and takes it to the window-sill and sits it outside, and she stands and looks at it a long moment. Then she closes the window, straightens her body with effort and turns to her children*)

MAMA Well—ain't it a mess in here, though? (*A false cheerfulness, a beginning of something*) I guess we all better stop moping around and get some work done. All this unpacking and everything we got to do. (RUTH *raises her head slowly in response to the sense of the line; and* BENEATHA *in similar manner turns very slowly to look at her mother*) One of you all better call the moving people and tell 'em not to come.

RUTH Tell 'em not to come?

MAMA Of course, baby. Ain't no need in 'em coming all the way here and having to go back. They charges for that too. (*She sits down, fingers to her brow, thinking*) Lord, ever since I was a little girl, I always remembers people saying, "Lena—Lena Eggleston, you aims too high all the time. You needs to slow down and see life a little more like it is. Just slow down some." That's what they always used to say down home—"Lord, that Lena Eggleston is a high-minded thing. She'll get her due one day!"

RUTH No, Lena . . .

MAMA Me and Big Walter didn't never learn right.

RUTH Lena, no! We gotta go. Bennie—tell her . . . (*She rises and crosses to* BENEATHA *with her arms out stretched.* BENEATHA *doesn't respond*) Tell her we can still move . . . the notes ain't but a hundred and twenty-five a month. We got four grown people in this house—we can work . . .

MAMA (*To herself*) Just aimed too high all the time—

RUTH (*Turning and going to* MAMA *fast—the words pouring out with urgency and desperation*) Lena—I'll work . . . I'll work twenty hours a day in the kitchens in Chicago . . . I'll strap my baby on my back if I have to and scrub all the floors in America and wash all the sheets in America if I have to—but we got to MOVE! We got to get OUT OF HERE!!

(MAMA *reaches out absently and pats* RUTH'S *hand*)

MAMA No—I sees things differently now. Been thinking 'bout some of the things we could do to fix this place up some. I seen a secondhand bureau over on Maxwell Street just the other day that could fit right there. (*She points to where the new furniture might go.* RUTH *wanders away from her*) Would need some new handles on it and then a little varnish and it look like something brand-new. And—we can put up them new curtains in the kitchen . . . Why this place be looking fine. Cheer us all up so that we forget trouble ever come . . . (*To* RUTH) And you could get some nice screens to put up in your room 'round the baby's bassinet . . . (*She looks at both of them, pleadingly*) Sometimes you just got to know when to give up some things . . . and hold on to what you got . . .

(WALTER *enters from the outside, looking spent and leaning against the door, his coat hanging from him*)

MAMA Where you been, son?

WALTER (*Breathing hard*) Made a call.

MAMA To who, son?

WALTER To The Man. (*He heads for his room*)

MAMA What man, baby?

WALTER (*Stops in the door*) The Man, Mama. Don't you know who The Man is?

RUTH Walter Lee?

WALTER *The Man.* Like the guys in the streets say—The Man. Captain Boss—Mistuh Charley . . . Old Cap'n Please Mr. Bossman . . .

BENEATHA (*Suddenly*) Lindner!

WALTER That's right! That's good. I told him to come right over.

BENEATHA (*Fiercely, understanding*) We going to do business with him.

MAMA What you talking 'bout, son?

WALTER Talking 'bout life, Mama. You all always telling me to see life like it is. Well—I laid in there on my back today . . . and I figured it out. Life just like it is. Who gets and who don't get. (*He sits down with his coat on and laughs*) Mama, you know it's all divided up. Life is. Sure enough. Between the takers and the "tooken." (*He laughs*) I've figured it out finally. (*He looks around at them*) Yeah. Some of us always getting "tooken." (*He laughs*) People like Willy Harris, they don't never get "tooken." And you know why the rest of us do? 'Cause we all mixed up. Mixed up bad. We get to looking 'round for the right and the wrong; and we worry about it and cry about it and stay up nights trying to figure out 'bout the wrong and the right of things all the time . . . And all the time, man, them takers is our there operating, just taking and taking. Willy Harris? Shoot—Willy Harris don't even count. He don't even count in the big scheme of things. But I'll say one thing for old Willy Harris . . . he's taught me something. He's taught me to keep my eye on what counts in this world. Yeah—(*Shouting out a little*) Thanks, Willy!

RUTH What did you call that man for, Walter Lee?

WALTER Called him to tell him to come on over to the show. Gonna put on a show for the man. Just what he wants to see. You see, Mama, the man came here today and he told us that them people out there where you want us to move—well they so upset they willing to pay us *not* to move! (*He laughs again*) And—and oh, Mama you would have been proud of the way me and Ruth and Bennie acted. We told him to get out . . . Lord have mercy! We told the man to get out! Oh, we was some proud folks this afternoon, yeah. (*He lights a cigarette*) We were still full of that old-time stuff . . .

RUTH (*Coming toward him slowly*) You talking 'bout taking them people's money to keep us from moving in that house?

WALTER I ain't just talking 'bout it, baby—I'm telling you that's what's going to happen!

BENEATHA Oh, God! Where is the bottom! Where is the real honest-to-God bottom so he can't go any farther!

WALTER See—that's the old stuff. You and that boy that was here today. You all want everybody to carry a flag and a spear and sing some marching songs, huh? You wanna spend your life looking into things and trying to find the right and the wrong part, huh? Yeah. You know what's going to happen to that boy someday—he'll find himself sitting in a dungeon, locked in forever—and the takers will have the key! Forget it, baby! There ain't no causes—there ain't nothing but taking in this world, and he who takes the most is smartest—and it don't make a damn bit of difference *how*.

MAMA You making something inside me cry, son. Some awful pain inside me.

WALTER Don't cry, Mama. Understand. The white man is going to walk in that door able to write checks for more money than we ever had. It's important to him and I'm going to help him . . . I'm going to put on the show, Mama.

MAMA Son—I come from five generations of people who was slaves and sharecroppers—but ain't nobody in my family never let nobody pay 'em no money that was a way of telling us we wasn't fit to walk the earth. We ain't never been that poor. (*Raising her eyes and looking at him*) We ain't never been that—dead inside.

BENEATHA Well—we are dead now. All the talk about dreams and sunlight that goes on in this house. It's all dead now.

WALTER What's the matter with you all! I didn't make this world! It was give to me this way! Hell, yes, I want me some yachts someday! Yes, I want to hang some real pearls 'round my wife's neck. Ain't she supposed to wear no pearls? Somebody tell me—tell me, who decides which women is supposed to wear pearls in this world. I tell you I am a *man*—and I think my wife should wear some pearls in this world!

(This last line hangs a good while and WALTER *begins to move about the room. The word "Man" has penetrated his consciousness; he mumbles it to himself repeatedly between strange agitated pauses as he moves about)*

MAMA Baby, how you going to feel on the inside?

WALTER Fine! . . . Going to feel fine . . . a man . . .

MAMA You won't have nothing left then, Walter Lee.

WALTER *(Coming to her)* I'm going to feel fine, Mama. I'm going to look that son-of-a-bitch in the eyes and say—*(He falters)*—and say, "All right, Mr. Lindner—*(He falters even more)*—that's *your* neighborhood out there! You got the right to keep it like you want! You got the right to have it like you want! Just write the check and—the house is yours." And—and I am going to say—*(His voice almost breaks)* "And you—you people just put the money in my hand and you won't have to live next to this bunch of stinking niggers! . . ." *(He straightens up and moves away from his mother, walking around the room)* And maybe—maybe I'll just get down on my black knees . . . *(He does so;* RUTH *and* BENNIE *and* MAMA *watch him in frozen horror)* "Captain, Mistuh, Bossman—*(Groveling and grinning and wringing his hands in profoundly anguished imitation of the slow-witted movie stereotype)* A-hee-hee-hee! Oh, yassuh boss! Yassssssuh! Great white—*(Voice breaking, he forces himself to go on)*—Father, just gi' ussen de money, fo' God's sake, and we's—we's ain't gwine come out deh and dirty up yo' white folks neighborhood . . ." *(He breaks down completely)* And I'll feel fine! Fine! FINE! *(He gets up and goes into the bedroom)*

BENEATHA That is not a man. That is nothing but a toothless rat.

MAMA Yes—death done come in this here house. *(She is nodding, slowly, reflectively)* Done come walking in my house on the lips of my children. You what supposed to be my beginning again. You—what supposed to be my harvest. *(To* BENEATHA*)* You—you mourning your brother?

BENEATHA He's no brother of mine.

MAMA What you say?

BENEATHA I said that that individual in that room is no brother of mine.

MAMA That's what I thought you said. You feeling like you better than he is today? *(*BENEATHA *does not answer)* Yes? What you tell him a minute ago? That he wasn't a man? Yes? You give him up for me? You done wrote his epitaph too—like the rest of the world? Well, who give you the privilege?

BENEATHA Be on my side for once! You saw what he just did, Mama! You saw him—down on his knees. Wasn't it you who taught me to despise any man who would do that? Do what he's going to do?

MAMA Yes—I taught you that. Me and your daddy. But I thought I taught you something else too . . . I thought I taught you to love him.

BENEATHA Love him? There is nothing left to love.

MAMA There is *always* something left to love. And if you ain't learned that, you ain't learned nothing. (*Looking at her*) Have you cried for that boy today? I don't mean for yourself and for the family 'cause we lost the money. I mean for him: what he been through and what it done to him. Child, when do you think is the time to love somebody the most? When they done good and made things easy for everybody? Well then, you ain't through learning—because that ain't the time at all. It's when he's at his lowest and can't believe in hisself 'cause the world done whipped him so! When you starts measuring somebody, measure him right, child, measure him right. Make sure you done taken into account what hills and valleys he come through before he got to wherever he is.

(TRAVIS *bursts into the room at the end of the speech, leaving the door open*)

TRAVIS Grandmama—the moving men are downstairs! The truck just pulled up.

MAMA (*Turning and looking at him*) Are they, baby? They downstairs?

(*She sighs and sits.* LINDNER *appears in the doorway. He peers in and knocks lightly, to gain attention, and comes in. All turn to look at him*)

LINDNER (*Hat and briefcase in hand*) Uh—hello . . .

(RUTH *crosses mechanically to the bedroom door and opens it and lets it swing open freely and slowly as the lights come up on* WALTER *within, still in his coat, sitting at the far corner of the room. He looks up and out through the room to* LINDNER)

RUTH He's here.

(*A long minute passes and* WALTER *slowly gets up*)

LINDNER (*Coming to the table with efficiency, putting his briefcase on the table and starting to unfold papers and unscrew fountain pens*) Well, I certainly was glad to hear from you people. (WALTER *has begun the trek out of the room, slowly and awkwardly, rather like a small boy, passing the back of his sleeve across his mouth from time to time*) Life can really be so much simpler than people let it be most of the time. Well—with whom do I negotiate? You, Mrs. Younger, or your son here? (MAMA *sits with her hands folded on her lap and her eyes closed as* WALTER *advances.* TRAVIS *goes closer to* LINDNER *and looks at the papers curiously*) Just some official papers, sonny.

RUTH Travis, you go downstairs—

MAMA (*Opening her eyes and looking into* WALTER'S) No. Travis, you stay right here. And you make him understand what you doing, Walter Lee. You teach him good. Like Willy Harris taught you. You show where our five generations done come to. (WALTER *looks from her to the boy, who grins at him innocently*) Go ahead, son—(*She folds her hands and closes her eyes*) Go ahead.

WALTER (*At last crosses to* LINDNER, *who is reviewing the contract*) Well, Mr. Lindner. (BENEATHA *turns away*) We called you—(*There is a profound, simple groping quality in his speech*)—because, well, me and my family (*He looks around and shifts from one foot to the other*) Well—we are very plain people . . .

LINDNER Yes—

WALTER I mean—I have worked as a chauffeur most of my life—and my wife here, she does domestic work in people's kitchens. So does my mother. I mean—we are plain people . . .

LINDNER Yes, Mr. Younger—

WALTER (*Really like a small boy, looking down at his shoes and then up at the man*) And—uh—well, my father, well, he was a laborer most of his life . . .

LINDNER (*Absolutely confused*) Uh, yes—yes, I understand. (*He turns back to the contract*)

WALTER (*A beat; staring at him*) And my father—(*With sudden intensity*) My father almost *beat a man to death* once because this man called him a bad name or something, you know what I mean?

LINDNER (*Looking up, frozen*) No, no, I'm afraid I don't—

WALTER (*A beat. The tension hangs; then* WALTER *steps back from it*) Yeah. Well—what I mean is that we come from people who had a lot of *pride*. I mean—we are very proud people. And that's my sister over there and she's going to be a doctor—and we are very proud—

LINDNER Well—I am sure that is very nice, but—

WALTER   What I am telling you is that we called you over here to tell you that we are very proud and that this—(*Signaling to* TRAVIS) Travis, come here. (TRAVIS *crosses and* WALTER *draws him before him facing the man*) This is my son, and he makes the sixth generation our family in this country. And we have all thought about your offer—

LINDNER   Well, good . . . good—

WALTER   And we have decided to move into our house because my father—my father—he earned it for us brick by brick. (MAMA *has her eyes closed and is rocking back and forth as though she were in church, with her head nodding the Amen yes*) We don't want to make no trouble for nobody or fight no causes, and we will try to be good neighbors. And that's *all* we got to say about that. (*He looks the man absolutely in the eyes*) We don't want your money. (*He turns and walks away*)

LINDNER   (*Looking around at all of them*) I take it then—that you have decided to occupy . . .

BENEATHA   That's what the man said.

LINDNER   (*To* MAMA *in her reverie*) Then I would like to appeal to you, Mrs. Younger. You are older and wiser and understand things better I am sure . . .

MAMA   I am afraid you don't understand. My son said we was going to move and there ain't nothing left for me to say. (*Briskly*) You know how these young folks is nowadays, mister. Can't do a thing with 'em! (*As he opens his mouth, she rises*) Good-bye.

LINDNER   (*Folding up his materials*) Well—if you are that final about it . . . there is nothing left for me to say. (*He finishes, almost ignored by the family, who are concentrating on* WALTER LEE. *At the door* LINDNER *halts and looks around*) I sure hope you people know what you're getting into.

(*He shakes his head and exits*)

RUTH   (*Looking around and coming to life*) Well, for God's sake—if the moving men are here—LET'S GET THE HELL OUT OF HERE!

MAMA   (*Into action*) Ain't it the truth! Look at all this here mess. Ruth, put Travis' good jacket on him . . . Walter Lee, fix your tie and tuck your shirt in, you look like somebody's hoodlum! Lord have mercy, where is my plant? (*She flies to get it amid the general bustling of the family, who are deliberately trying to ignore the nobility of the past moment*) You all start on down . . . Travis child, don't go empty-handed . . . Ruth, where did I put that box with my skillets in it? I want to be in charge of it myself . . . I'm going to make us the biggest dinner we ever ate tonight . . . Beneatha, what's the matter with them stockings? Pull them things up, girl . . .

(*The family starts to file out as two moving men appear and begin to carry out the heavier pieces of furniture, bumping into the family as they move about*)

BENEATHA   Mama, Asagai asked me to marry him today and go to Africa—

MAMA   (*In the middle of her getting-ready activity*) He did? You ain't old enough to marry nobody—(*Seeing the moving men lifting one of her chairs precariously*) Darling, that ain't no bale of cotton, please handle it so we can sit in it again! I had that chair twenty-five years . . .

(*The movers sigh with exasperation and go on with their work*)

BENEATHA   (*Girlishly and unreasonably trying to pursue the conversation*) To go to Africa, Mama—be a doctor in Africa . . .

MAMA   (*Distracted*) Yes, baby—

WALTER   *Africa!* What he want you to go to Africa for?

BENEATHA   To practice there . . .

WALTER   Girl, if you don't get all them silly ideas out your head! You better marry yourself a man with some loot . . .

BENEATHA   (*Angrily, precisely as in the first scene of the play*) What have you got to do with who I marry!

WALTER   Plenty. Now I think George Murchison—

BENEATHA   *George Murchison!* I wouldn't marry him if he was Adam and I was Eve!

(WALTER *and* BENEATHA *go out yelling at each other vigorously and the anger is loud and real till their voices diminish.* RUTH *stands at the door and turns to* MAMA *and smiles knowingly*)

MAMA   (*Fixing her hat at last*) Yeah—they something all right, my children . . .

RUTH   Yes—they're something. Let's go, Lena.

MAMA   (*Stalling, starting to look around at the house*) Yes—I'm coming. Ruth—

RUTH   Yes?

MAMA   (*Quietly, woman to woman*) He finally come into his manhood today, didn't he? Kind of like a rainbow after the rain . . .

RUTH (*Biting her lip lest her own pride explode in front of* MAMA) Yes, Lena.

(WALTER'S *voice calls for them raucously*)

WALTER (*Off stage*) Y'all come on! These people charges by the hour, you know!

MAMA (*Waving* RUTH *out vaguely*) All right, honey—go on down. I be down directly.

(RUTH *hesitates, then exits.* MAMA *stands, at last alone in the living room, her plant on the table before her as the lights start to come down. She looks around at all the walls and ceilings and suddenly, despite herself, while the children call below, a great heaving thing rises in her and she puts her fist to her mouth to stiffle it, takes a final desperate look, pulls her coat about her, pats her hat and goes out. The lights dim down. The door opens and she comes back in, grabs her plant, and goes out for the last time*)

Curtain

Related Readings

Spike Lee

Commentary: Thoughts on the Screenplay

Filmmaker Spike Lee explores all aspects of the African American experience in his work. In this essay, he shares his ideas about Lorraine Hansberry's unfilmed original screenplay for A Raisin in the Sun.

HISTORY is an important word, an important concept, but today it seems like this particular word is foreign to a lot of us African Americans. The history I'm talking about is not ancient African history either; it's recent history. If you polled all the black players in the NBA, I'd bet my left arm only a couple could tell you who was the first black player in the league. The same with the NFL; a greater percentage would know about Jackie Robinson being the first in baseball, but there still might be some who didn't have a clue. (I choose these examples because I'm an avid sports fan, but the same results would be evident across the board. Young African American kids know the names of Martin Luther King, Jr., and Malcolm X, but it's a very superficial knowledge.) A lot of us are again clueless about Ms. Hansberry.

It's time to include Lorraine Hansberry in those history lessons. Reading her original screenplay of *A Raisin in the Sun* was a revelation for me. I had seen the movie on television, but I was too young to have seen the Broadway production (I would have probably liked it better than the film). Like all great works of art, this stuff doesn't get old. And for me *Raisin* is still fresh, it's still relevant. Lorraine Hansberry was a visionary.

Today, everybody and their mother are talking about "Afrocentricity." But Hansberry was writing about it long before it became fashionable. ("Hell no, don't call me no African! I'm a Negro, I'm colored, etc., etc." We've all heard that numerous times.) For me, the brilliance of *Raisin* is the examination of the African American family. And we all have to ask ourselves, have things gotten any better than when the play was written? I have to say I think they've gotten worse. We've made some advances as a people, but our families have gotten weaker. Back in the day when Lorraine wrote this play, we did not have the astronomical amount of teenage mothers, the drugs, the black-on-black crime, young black males dying at one another's hands, the miseducation of black youth, and so on. This is a big part of the reason why we're in the sorry state we're in. The black family structure is at an all-time low.

But with this recent so-called "explosion" of black cinema, the names most repeated are Oscar Micheaux, Gordon Parks, Ossie Davis, and Melvin Van Peebles. From this day on, I'm going to start to include Ms. Hansberry. Her play is a landmark in American theater, and in the right hands, the film could have been a landmark in cinema. (Regardless, it still stands as an important piece.) One sees the freedom she had with the play that Hollywood, or in this specific case, Columbia Pictures, wasn't having.

After I finished reading the screenplay, I went out and rented the video cassette. It seems to me all the cuts had to deal with softening a too defiant black voice. I found the parts that were cut to be some of the most interesting parts of the screenplay. Of course, Columbia probably cited length as the reason for the deletions. But I feel Lorraine was right in her vision to "open up" the play. She just didn't want to film a *play*; *she wanted to make it cinematic, to make it a film*. In the final result, the film is very stagey. It's my guess that once she signed her deal, she had very little say on how the project would be realized. And it was a triumph for her to write the screenplay and get the film made.

You might ask, what would Hansberry have done if she hadn't been taken away from us so soon? I'd like to think that *Raisin* would have been her first of many fine screenplays. Can you name another African American female who has written a screenplay for a Hollywood studio that got made? I cannot.

The history must be taught, and if not in the schools then at home. But that won't or can't be done until our home life, our families, get back on track. It's a vicious cycle. We still have a long, long way to go.

Susan Sinnott

The Human Race Concerns Me . . .

To truly understand and appreciate some works of artistic expression, it is important to understand the historical context in which they were created.

HOST: Are there any particular themes that concern you as a dramatist? Or is it more general?

L. H.: The human race concerns me and everything that implies. . . .

—Lorraine Hansberry,
To Be Young, Gifted, and Black

DURING THE TIME that Lorraine was writing her play, America was in the happy grip of a new form of entertainment—television. Many Americans spent hours every week watching the small black-and-white screen that sat inside a big paneled box. They laughed at the bright clown *Howdy Doody* and at *I Love Lucy*, cried at dramas on *Hallmark Hall of Fame*, and grew increasingly angry at news footage from places like Alabama, Mississippi, and Arkansas. The civil rights movement was the first major ongoing story to be covered by television.

In December 1955, Rosa Parks, a department store seamstress in Montgomery, Alabama, boarded a bus at the end of a long workday and took a seat in the back. A few stops later, the bus was full. Since by law any black person was obligated to give their seat to any white person, Rosa was asked by the bus driver to leave her seat. She refused. She was tired, she explained, she'd paid her fare, and she intended to stay seated until she got to her stop. Rosa, whose unassuming manner masked a steely determination, was arrested and taken to jail. Within a few days, a group of civil rights activists, including a young Baptist minister named Martin Luther King, Jr., organized a boycott of the Montgomery bus system. This thirteen-month-long boycott was characterized by crude and violent behavior by Montgomery's white citizens. America watched it all on television with growing fascination.

In the fall of 1957, nine black students attempted to begin classes at Little Rock's all-white Central High School. The landmark Supreme Court decision *Brown v. Topeka* (or *Brown v. Board of Education*, as it is more commonly known) made school segregation illegal; yet, in the South, integration of local schools was achieved only by force and on a school-by-school basis. When the nine students attempted to enter Central High, the Governor of Arkansas called out the Arkansas National Guard to block their entrance. President Eisenhower could not allow a state to block enforcement of a Supreme Court ruling, so he sent in 1,000 Army troops to escort the students to school. As the students walked past white demonstrators, they were pelted with eggs, taunted, and jeered. The rest of America watched on television.

When these scenes of violence and hatred came into the living rooms of ordinary people, the viewers were changed forever. White Americans had heard about the treatment of blacks by Southerners, but now that they were confronted with it on television, they felt outrage, sympathy, and guilt. Many were roused from complacency and began to wish for an end to the unjust and unnecessary suffering.

As Arkansas Governor Orval Faubus announced on nationwide television that he would do nothing to protect the black students at Central High School, Lorraine completed the first draft of *A Raisin in the Sun*. One evening a short while later, she and Robert invited an old friend, Burt D'Lugoff, Robert's "Cindy, Oh, Cindy" collaborator, and Philip Rose, a music publisher, to dinner at their apartment. Lorraine made spaghetti and served banana cream pie, and then, when the table was cleared and Spice, their "sort of collie," was locked in the bedroom to prevent interruption, she began to read her play. Lorraine remembered feeling that during that evening she gave birth to the play; it left her body and took on a life of its own. When she was done, the four talked long into the night. By the time D'Lugoff and Rose left the apartment, at nearly daybreak, they were planning how to take *A Raisin in the Sun* to Broadway.

To say the least, mounting a full-scale Broadway production for a black drama written by an unknown black woman was a remote possibility. Broadway audiences were nearly 100 percent white and any roles for blacks had been strictly for their value as "exotic entertainment," as defined by whites. (One notable exception had been the work of Paul Robeson, who appeared on Broadway in Shakespeare's *Othello* and Eugene O'Neill's *All*

God's Chillun Got Wings and *The Emperor Jones*.) The idea that blacks might have problems with which whites could empathize was so new as to seem radical. That black people themselves might come to the theater to see such a play was unimaginable. As James Baldwin said, "Black people ignored the theater because the theater had always ignored them."

All of this made *A Raisin in the Sun* seem extremely risky to potential investors. Philip Rose, however, was so smitten with the play that within days of Lorraine's reading he contacted his friend, the stage and film actor Sidney Poitier, about the role of Walter Lee Younger. Poitier, who had recently starred in the films *Cry, the Beloved Country*, *The Blackboard Jungle*, and *The Defiant Ones*, was moved by the part. Calling Lorraine's "fix on the black experience truly uncanny," he agreed at once. He told Philip Rose that he knew of a possible director, a talented young black man named Lloyd Richards. Before long, Ruby Dee, who had played opposite Sidney Poitier in the film *The Edge of Night* and who was a friend of Lorraine's and Bob's, was cast as Ruth Younger, and the veteran actress Claudia McNeil took the role of Mama.

Despite assembling an impressive cast, the producers had to go to extraordinary lengths to secure financing. After being turned down by every established backer in the theater business, Robert Nemiroff, Burt D'Lugoff, and another newcomer, David Cogan, used a network of friends and acquaintances, all of whom helped usher *A Raisin in the Sun* through a maze of union laws and rehearsal restrictions. Large investors were not to be found; instead, they asked a total of 147 individuals, including such well-known black artists as Harry Belafonte, to contribute $250 each. Even with the money in hand, no Broadway theater would consider even renting space to the production.

Still, there was considerable excitement, both within the production and gradually among the New York theater community as well, about the sparkling script and the talented cast and crew. Rehearsal began in New York on December 27, 1958, and a month later, the company was ready for tryouts in New Haven. Despite the sense of, as one reporter noted, "an emerging bombshell," all was not harmonious behind the scenes. Just as Lorraine had wavered on paper about whether Mama or Walter Lee should be the play's main character, so Sidney Poitier and Claudia McNeil had their own ideas on the matter. Sidney wanted Walter Lee to dominate; not surprisingly, Claudia McNeil's Mama jockeyed for the same position. Lloyd Richards, Phil Rose, and Lorraine were happy with Mama's dominance on the stage and, judging from the first reactions in New Haven, audiences agreed. Sidney Poitier's objections, however, were ironclad. He believed that if the play unfolded from Mama's point of view, Walter Lee would be weakened to the point that his character would reflect badly on all black males. He felt this so strongly, he wrote later, that he reworked his entire performance so he could play against, rather than cower before, Claudia McNeil's powerful Mama.

Lorraine tried to see Sidney's point but insisted she had not purposely written a weak male role. The glowing reviews in New Haven and then in Philadelphia hardened Lorraine, Phil, and Lloyd's resolve to "lock the play in," to call its form final. Sidney protested, and Lorraine ultimately accused him of behaving like an impetuous star who didn't want to share the audience's attention with another actor. Sidney, for his part, accused Lorraine and the producers of "smelling gold" and being reluctant to make reasonable artistic changes. The arguments lasted for hours, Sidney remembered, and eventually, he and Lorraine stopped speaking altogether.

As Robert Nemiroff wrote many years later, "The pressures were enormous (if unspoken and rarely even acknowledged in the excitement of the work) not to press fate unduly with unnecessary risks." The sacrifices— whole scenes were cut—were made simply to keep the play at a length that would be acceptable to investors and theatergoers alike. When audiences reacted warmly to Mama's character, Lorraine and the others were inclined to leave her alone.

Despite the glowing reviews in New Haven and Philadelphia, a Broadway theater was not immediately available, so the Schubert organization, which now wished to book *A Raisin in the Sun* in its Ethel Barrymore Theatre, suggested a run in Chicago. Philip Rose and David Cogan accepted the offer, and Lorraine prepared to go back to her   and to *Raisin's*— home, this time as an "almost celebrity."

By the time the play arrived in Chicago, *A Raisin in the Sun's* success seemed all but assured. Sidney Poitier's grumbling faded a bit, and Claudia McNeil, whose contract lasted as long as the play's New York run, allowed herself to think that the play might run for months and months. Lorraine couldn't think that far ahead. She could only think "Chicago," where the audience would be full of friends and family.

Lorraine's sister, Mamie, remembered that when people spoke of the play—and during those days who could talk of anything else?—their mother would just nod her head and beam. Yet privately her daughter's stunning success seemed to bring tears as often as smiles, tears of joy and of sadness, too. How Carl would have enjoyed this moment, she couldn't help but think, and how it would have eased some of the pain of those long-ago years when the family moved to Washington Park. At that time neither Carl nor Nannie could have known how that experience would affect their children's lives, much less that their youngest would one day pour her fear and emotional anguish into a work of art.

On opening night, Lorraine, dressed, styled, and made up to Mamie's total satisfaction, thought about Carl too. She felt his presence everywhere in the theater, not just in the plot and words of the play, but also in the knowing smiles and warm hugs of their friends. When, in the final scene, Walter Lee says with conviction: "And we have decided to move into our house because my father—my father—he earned it for us brick by brick. . . ," Lorraine could hear gasps and sobs around her as these people—*her* people—recognized themselves in Walter's words. "We don't want to make no trouble for nobody or fight no causes and we will try to be good neighbors. And that's *all* we got to say about that. . . ."

Lorraine, sitting with Nannie and Mamie, squeezed her mother's hand as the curtain fell. She didn't let go until the audience jumped to its feet and Lorraine, pulled from her seat, acknowledged their approval with a wave. Then the faces closed in around her and seemed to become part of a dizzying blur. She struggled to focus her eyes and make out familiar features. Where are you, Langston? she wondered. I heard you were coming tonight, how I would love to see your face! And, what about the others from the early days—Pale Hecate, Mamie's football player, the kids on the school playground who poured ink on her white fur coat? Suddenly, the house lights came up and the faces near by, in full color now, began to speak: *We just loved it. . . . Thank you, dear, thank you. . . . You captured our experience, our lives, and now the whole world will want to see. . . .*

"The Tuesday night it opened in Chicago," remembered Chicago journalist Lerone Bennett, "that was one of the most delightful evenings I've ever spent in the theater. The play . . . the *people* . . . All that richness, all that great talent on one stage . . . the totality packed a wallop."

Later that night, Mr. Bennett attended a reception at the Hansberry home. "It was that kind of party, you know, . . . an emerging celebrity, Chicago girl, and old Chicago people who hadn't seen her in a long time. . . . She was being transformed from an anonymous person into a celebrity." It wasn't a time for serious talk, as Lorraine whirled from one cluster of friends to another. They all wanted to share this moment with her, and she in turn wanted to thank them for coming, and for their support. In the end, though, after the well-wishers left, Lorraine flopped down on the couch and talked with the few remaining guests about "art and struggle" and all that she wanted to do in the future. Except, of course, at that moment, Lorraine Hansberry's future was absolutely unpredictable.

As Lorraine headed back to New York and the Broadway opening of *A Raisin in the Sun*, she couldn't help but wonder what all this—this becoming famous—would mean for her life. Of course she wanted fame, but, for example, when was the last time she'd been alone with her husband? As a producer and partner, he'd been along for this wild ride, too; yet what were his thoughts? Clearly, *Raisin* had control of both their lives and would keep it for much longer. Lorraine couldn't help but feel a twinge of anxiety. Would life together with Bob ever be the same? Could she try to hold on to what she didn't want to change?

On March 11, when the play finally opened at the Ethel Barrymore Theatre, Lorraine sat in the audience again, with her mother, sister, brothers, and their families. She wore the stunning black dress Mamie had insisted she buy in Chicago. Scattered throughout the theater were fellow artists, writers, activists, and—most importantly for Lorraine—ordinary people, black and white, who had come to see her little play. They came, as James Baldwin wrote, "because the life on that stage said something to them concerning their own lives."

As the curtain came down on the third act, the audience members rose to their feet so spontaneously and boisterously that many in the cast were moved to tears. Director Lloyd Richards walked onto the stage and then the clapping became a steady beat, and shouts of 'Author, author, author," were heard throughout the theater. Ruby Dee leaned over and asked Sidney Poitier to lead Lorraine up to the stage from the audience. He jumped down and brought her from her mother's side. Standing among the cast, looking small and slightly dazed, she wasn't sure herself whether to laugh or cry.

Early that morning, the tired, giddy cast and crew gathered to read the reviews:

"It is honest drama," wrote Frank Aston in the *New York World Telegram*. "Catching up real people. It may rip you to shreds. It will make you proud of human beings." "There is nothing more moving in *A Raisin in the Sun*," wrote Walter Kerr in the *New York Herald Tribune*, "than the spectacle of Sidney Poitier biting his lip, clutching the back of a chair, and turning himself into a man." "The play is honest," added Brooks Atkinson of the *New York Times*. "It is Miss Hansberry's personal contribution to an explosive situation in which simple honesty is the most difficult thing in the world. And also the most illuminating."

The timing for *Raisin*'s appearance on the national scene couldn't have been better. The civil rights movement, with Martin Luther King, Jr. as its leader, had grabbed headlines around the world. Young black students, emboldened by the actions of Rosa Parks and the Little Rock Nine, had begun to organize and stage protests and sit-ins throughout the South. They were proudly following in the footsteps of Frederick Douglass, W. E. B. DuBois, and Paul Robeson. They, like Walter Lee Younger, wanted only to be treated with ordinary human dignity.

The sit-ins and protests drew the usual response from Southern politicians and police. Students were arrested, expelled from school. One young man was kidnapped, whipped, and had the Ku Klux Klan symbol carved on his abdomen. Others were attacked by police dogs and struck by clubs and chains. Broadcast on television day after day, the images gripped the American public. It seemed too much sometimes, enough to make some whites wonder: Were they capable of such things themselves?

At the same time, both whites and blacks flocked to see *A Raisin in the Sun*, both at its out-of-town tryouts and on Broadway. Blue-collar workers from Harlem, Brooklyn, and the Bronx joined society matrons from Westchester County. How they loved Mama, as portrayed by Claudia McNeil, who had such an ability "to tweak the heartstrings," as one reviewer noted. Sidney Poitier as Walter Lee was "noble" and "heroic," and the entire ensemble "stunning."

Audiences watched a full evening of the heartbreaks and triumphs of a black family and when they left the theater they felt good—about themselves and about the world. They were surprised, and pleased, by their own reactions. Why, the Youngers were just like any other family! And Mama— wise, exasperating, loving—was just like their own sweet mothers. At first, Lorraine was delighted by the praise and attention, but she soon grew troubled. Many whites seemed to take these warm feelings as proof that they themselves were just fine, that, yes, there were mean people who would treat the Youngers badly, but that didn't include *them*. Why, not only had they enjoyed the play, but they'd actually identified with the characters— black characters! Didn't that make them less guilty of racial intolerance than most everyone else? Certainly less than those terrible people on television, the ones who set dogs and firehoses on defenseless black people?

In an effort to recover *Raisin*'s original message—that all people, no matter how downtrodden, have within them "the very essence of human dignity," and to push the play's audience to understand the larger issues of racial justice, she decided to include major changes in the screenplay for the film version, which she had agreed to write. Random House wanted to publish the script later the same year, and Lorraine would insist they include the scenes and sections cut during the rehearsal period. These inclusions, she believed, would make the Youngers' ongoing struggle against racism all the more immediate and powerful. Lorraine also vowed to use the many interviews she granted to, in effect, plead the Youngers' case again. As she set to work, it almost seemed to Lorraine that after having seen her brilliant child through its birth, infancy, and childhood, now, just when she thought *A Raisin in the Sun* would stand on its own, it needed her more than ever.

Langston Hughes

Deferred

*Langston Hughes was known as the Poet Laureate of
Black America. Hughes once described the subjects of his
work as "people up today and down tomorrow, working
this week and fired the next, beaten and baffled, but
determined not to be wholly beaten."*

This year, maybe, do you think I can graduate?
I'm already two years late.
Dropped out six months when I was seven,
a year when I was eleven,
5   then got put back when we come North.
To get through high at twenty's kind of late—
But maybe this year I can graduate.

Maybe now I can have that white enamel stove
I dreamed about when we first fell in love
10   eighteen years ago.
But you know,
rooming and everything
then kids,
cold-water flat and all that.
15   But now my daughter's married
And my boy's most grown—
quit school to work—
and where we're moving
there ain't no stove—
20   Maybe I can buy that white enamel stove!

Me, I always did want to study French.
It don't make sense—

I'll never go to France,
but night schools teach French.
25 *Now at last I've got a job*
where I get off at five,

in time to wash and dress,
so, s'il vous plaît, I'll study French!

Someday,
30 I'm gonna buy two new suits
at once!

All I want is
one more bottle of gin.

All I want is to see
35 my furniture paid for.

All I want is a wife who will
work with me and not against me. Say,
baby, could you see your way clear?

Heaven, heaven, is my home!
40 This world I'll leave behind
When I set my feet in glory
I'll have a throne for mine!

I want to pass the civil service.

I want a television set.

45 *You know, as old as I am,*
I ain't never
owned a decent radio yet?

I'd like to take up Bach.

Montage
50 *of a dream*
deferred.

Buddy, have you heard?

Langston Hughes

Note on Commercial Theatre

You've taken my blues and gone—
You sing 'em on Broadway
And you sing 'em in Hollywood Bowl,
And you mixed 'em up with symphonies

5　And you fixed 'em
So they don't sound like me.
Yep, you done taken my blues and gone.

You also took my spirituals and gone.
You put me in *Macbeth* and *Carmen Jones*
10　And all kinds of *Swing Mikados*
And in everything but what's about me—
But someday somebody'll
Stand up and talk about me,
And write about me—
15　Black and beautiful—
And sing about me,
And put on plays about me!
I reckon it'll be
Me myself!

20　Yes, it'll be me.

Alice Walker

Everyday Use

As seen in A Raisin in the Sun, *people within a family can have very different ideas about what their heritage means to them.*

I WILL WAIT FOR HER in the yard that Maggie and I made so clean and wavy yesterday afternoon. A yard like this is more comfortable than most people know. It is not just a yard. It is like an extended living room. When the hard clay is swept clean as a floor and the fine sand around the edges lined with tiny, irregular grooves, anyone can come and sit and look up into the elm tree and wait for the breezes that never come inside the house.

Maggie will be nervous until after her sister goes: she will stand hopelessly in corners, homely and ashamed of the burn scars down her arms and legs, eying her sister with a mixture of envy and awe. She thinks her sister has held life always in the palm of one hand, that "no" is a word the world never learned to say to her.

You've no doubt seen those TV shows where the child who has "made it" is confronted, as a surprise, by her own mother and father, tottering in weakly from backstage. (A pleasant surprise, of course: What would they do if parent and child came on the show only to curse out and insult each other?) On TV mother and child embrace and smile into each other's faces. Sometimes the mother and father weep, the child wraps them in her arms and leans across the table to tell how she would not have made it without their help. I have seen these programs.

Sometimes I dream a dream in which Dee and I are suddenly brought together on a TV program of this sort. Out of a dark and soft-seated limousine I am ushered into a bright room filled with many people. There I meet a smiling, gray, sporty man like Johnny Carson who shakes my hand and tells me what a fine girl I have. Then we are on the stage and Dee is embracing me with tears in her eyes. She pins on my dress a large orchid, even though she has told me once that she thinks orchids are tacky flowers.

In real life I am a large, big-boned woman with rough, man-working hands. In the winter I wear flannel nightgowns to bed and overalls during the day. I can kill and clean a hog as mercilessly as a man. My fat keeps me hot in zero weather. I can work outside all day, breaking ice to get water for washing; I can eat pork liver cooked over the open fire minutes after it comes steaming from the hog. One winter I knocked a bull calf straight in the brain between the eyes with a sledge hammer and had the meat hung up to chill before nightfall. But of course all this does not show on television. I am the way my daughter would want me to be: a hundred pounds lighter, my skin like an uncooked barley pancake. My hair glistens in the hot bright lights. Johnny Carson has much to do to keep up with my quick and witty tongue.

But that is a mistake. I know even before I wake up. Who ever knew a Johnson with a quick tongue? Who can even imagine me looking a strange white man in the eye? It seems to me I have talked to them always with one foot raised in flight, with my head turned in whichever way is farthest from them. Dee, though. She would always look anyone in the eye. Hesitation was no part of her nature.

"How do I look, Mama?" Maggie says, showing just enough of her thin body enveloped in pink skirt and red blouse for me to know she's there, almost hidden by the door.

"Come out into the yard," I say.

Have you ever seen a lame animal, perhaps a dog run over by some careless person rich enough to own a car, sidle up to someone who is ignorant enough to be kind to him? That is the way my Maggie walks. She has been like this, chin on chest, eyes on ground, feet in shuffle, ever since the fire that burned the other house to the ground.

Dee is lighter than Maggie, with nicer hair and a fuller figure. She's a woman now, though sometimes I forget. How long ago was it that the other house burned? Ten, twelve years? Sometimes I can still hear the flames and feel Maggie's arms sticking to me, her hair smoking and her dress falling off her in little black papery flakes. Her eyes seemed stretched open, blazed open by the flames reflected in them. And Dee. I see her standing off under the sweet gum tree she used to dig gum out of; a look of concentration on her face as she watched the last dingy gray board of the house fall in toward the red-hot brick chimney. Why don't you do a dance around the ashes? I'd wanted to ask her. She had hated the house that much.

I used to think she hated Maggie, too. But that was before we raised the money, the church and me, to send her to Augusta to school. She used to read to us without pity; forcing words, lies, other folks' habits, whole lives upon us two, sitting trapped and ignorant underneath her voice. She washed us in a river of make-believe, burned us with a lot of knowledge we didn't necessarily need to know. Pressed us to her with the serious way she read, to shove us away at just the moment, like dimwits, we seemed about to understand.

Dee wanted nice things. A yellow organdy dress to wear to her graduation from high school; black pumps to match a green suit she'd made from an old suit somebody gave me. She was determined to stare down any disaster in her efforts. Her eyelids would not flicker for minutes at a time. Often I fought off the temptation to shake her. At sixteen she had a style of her own: and knew what style was.

I never had an education myself. After second grade the school was closed down. Don't ask me why: in 1927 colored asked fewer questions than they do now. Sometimes Maggie reads to me. She stumbles along good-naturedly but can't see well. She knows she is not bright. Like good looks and money, quickness passed her by. She will marry John Thomas (who has mossy teeth in an earnest face) and then I'll be free to sit here and I guess just sing church songs to myself. Although I never was a good singer. Never could carry a tune. I was always better at a man's job. I used to love to milk till I was hooked in the side in '49. Cows are soothing and slow and don't bother you, unless you try to milk them the wrong way.

I have deliberately turned my back on the house. It is three rooms, just like the one that burned, except the roof is tin; they don't make shingle roofs any more. There are no real windows, just some holes cut in the sides, like the portholes in a ship, but not round and not square, with rawhide holding the shutters up on the outside. This house is in a pasture, too, like the other one. No doubt when Dee sees it she will want to tear it down. She wrote me once that no matter where we "choose" to live, she will manage to come see us. But she will never bring her friends. Maggie and I thought about this and Maggie asked me, "Mama, when did Dee ever *have* any friends?"

She had a few. Furtive boys in pink shirts hanging about on washday after school. Nervous girls who never laughed. Impressed with her they worshiped the well-turned phrase, the cute shape, the scalding humor that erupted like bubbles in lye. She read to them.

When she was courting Jimmy T she didn't have much time to pay to us, but turned all her faultfinding power on him. He *flew* to marry a cheap city girl from a family of ignorant flashy people. She hardly had time to recompose herself.

When she comes I will meet—but there they are!

Maggie attempts to make a dash for the house, in her shuffling way, but I stay her with my hand. "Come back here," I say. And she stops and tries to dig a well in the sand with her toe.

It is hard to see them clearly through the strong sun. But even the first glimpse of leg out of the car tells me it is Dee. Her feet were always neat-looking, as if God himself had shaped them with a certain style. From the other side of the car comes a short, stocky man. Hair is all over his head a foot long and hanging from his chin like a kinky mule tail. I hear Maggie suck in her breath. "Uhnnnh," is what it sounds like. Like when you see the wriggling end of a snake just in front of your foot on the road. "Uhnnnh."

Dee next. A dress down to the ground, in this hot weather. A dress so loud it hurts my eyes. There are yellows and oranges enough to throw back the light of the sun. I feel my whole face warming from the heat waves it throws out. Earrings gold, too, and hanging down to her shoulders. Bracelets dangling and making noises when she moves her arm up to shake the folds of the dress out of her armpits. The dress is loose and flows, and as she walks closer, I like it. I hear Maggie go "Uhnnnh" again. It is her sister's hair. It stands straight up like the wool on a sheep. It is black as night and around the edges are two long pigtails that rope about like small lizards disappearing behind her ears.

"Wa-su-zo-Tean-o!" she says, coming on in that gliding way the dress makes her move. The short stocky fellow with the hair to his navel is all grinning and follows up with "Asalamalakim, my mother and sister!" He moves to hug Maggie but she falls back, right up against the back of my chair. I feel her trembling there and when I look up I see the perspiration falling off her chin.

"Don't get up," says Dee. Since I am stout it takes something of a push. You can see me trying to move a second or two before I make it. She turns, showing white heels through her sandals, and goes back to the car. Out she peeks next with a Polaroid. She stoops down quickly and lines up picture after picture of me sitting there in front of the house with Maggie cowering behind me. She never takes a shot without making sure the house is included. When a cow comes nibbling around the edge of the yard she snaps it and me and Maggie *and* the house. Then she puts the Polaroid in the back seat of the car, and comes up and kisses me on the forehead.

Meanwhile Asalamalakim is going through motions with Maggie's hand. Maggie's hand is as limp as a fish, and probably as cold, despite the sweat, and she keeps trying to pull it back. It looks like Asalamalakim wants to shake hands but wants to do it fancy. Or maybe he don't know how people shake hands. Anyhow, he soon gives up on Maggie.

"Well," I say. "Dee."

"No, Mama," she says. "Not 'Dee,' Wangero Leewanika Kemanjo!"

"What happened to 'Dee'?" I wanted to know.

"She's dead," Wangero said. "I couldn't bear it any longer, being named after the people who oppress me."

"You know as well as me you was named after your aunt Dicie," I said. Dicie is my sister. She named Dee. We called her "Big Dee" after Dee was born.

"But who was *she* named after?" asked Wangero.

"I guess after Grandma Dee," I said.

"And who was she named after?" asked Wangero.

"Her mother," I said, and saw Wangero was getting tired. "That's about as far back as I can trace it," I said. Though, in fact, I probably could have carried it back beyond the Civil War through the branches.

"Well," said Asalamalakim, "there you are."

"Uhnnnh," I heard Maggie say.

"There I was not," I said, "before 'Dicie' cropped up in our family, so why should I try to trace it that far back?"

He just stood there grinning, looking down on me like somebody inspecting a Model A car. Every once in a while he and Wangero sent eye signals over my head.

"How do you pronounce this name?" I asked.

"You don't have to call me by it if you don't want to," said Wangero.

"Why shouldn't I?" I asked. "If that's what you want us to call you, we'll call you."

"I know it might sound awkward at first," said Wangero.

"I'll get used to it," I said. "Ream it out again."

Well, soon we got the name out of the way. Asalamalakim had a name twice as long and three times as hard. After I tripped over it two or three times he told me to just call him Hakim-a-barber. I wanted to ask him was he a barber, but I didn't really think he was, so I didn't ask.

"You must belong to those beef cattle peoples down the road," I said. They said "Asalamalakim" when they met you, too, but they didn't shake hands. Always too busy: feeding the cattle, fixing the fences, putting up salt-lick shelters, throwing down hay. When the white folks poisoned some of the herd the men stayed up all night with rifles in their hands. I walked a mile and a half just to see the sight.

Hakim-a-barber said, "I accept some of their doctrines, but farming and raising cattle is not my style." (They didn't tell me, and I didn't ask, whether Wangero (Dee) had really gone and married him.)

We sat down to eat and right away he said he didn't eat collards and pork was unclean. Wangero, though, went on through the chitlins and corn bread, the greens and everything else. She talked a blue streak over the sweet potatoes. Everything delighted her. Even the fact that we still used the benches her daddy made for the table when we couldn't afford to buy chairs.

"Oh, Mama!" she cried. Then turned to Hakim-a-barber. "I never knew how lovely these benches are. You can feel the rump prints," she said, running her hands underneath her and along the bench. Then she gave a sigh and her hand closed over Grandma Dee's butter dish. "That's it!" she said. "I knew there was something I wanted to ask you if I could have." She jumped up from the table and went over in the corner where the churn stood, the milk in it clabber by now. She looked at the churn and looked at it.

"This churn top is what I need," she said. "Didn't Uncle Buddy whittle it out of a tree you all used to have?"

"Yes," I said.

"Uh huh," she said happily. "And I want the dasher, too."

"Uncle Buddy whittle that, too?" asked the barber.

Dee (Wangero) looked up at me.

"Aunt Dee's first husband whittled the dash," said Maggie so low you almost couldn't hear her. "His name was Henry, but they called him Stash."

"Maggie's brain is like an elephant's," Wangero said, laughing. "I can use the churn top as a centerpiece for the alcove table," she said, sliding a plate over the churn, "and I'll think of something artistic to do with the dasher."

When she finished wrapping the dasher the handle stuck out. I took it for a moment in my hands. You didn't even have to look close to see where hands pushing the dasher up and down to make butter had left a kind of sink in the wood. In fact, there were a lot of small sinks; you could see where thumbs and fingers had sunk into the wood. It was beautiful light yellow wood, from a tree that grew in the yard where Big Dee and Stash had lived.

After dinner Dee (Wangero) went to the trunk at the foot of my bed and started rifling through it. Maggie hung back in the kitchen over the dishpan. Out came Wangero with two quilts. They had been pieced by Grandma Dee and then Big Dee and me had hung them on the quilt frames on the front porch and quilted them. One was in the Lone Star pattern. The other was Walk Around the Mountain. In both of them were scraps of dresses Grandma Dee had worn fifty and more years ago. Bits and pieces of Grandpa Jarrell's Paisley shirts. And one teeny faded blue piece, about the size of a penny matchbox, that was from Great Grandpa Ezra's uniform that he wore in the Civil War.

"Mama," Wangero said sweet as a bird. "Can I have these old quilts?"

I heard something fall in the kitchen, and a minute later the kitchen door slammed.

"Why don't you take one or two of the others?" I asked. "These old things was just done by me and Big Dee from some tops your grandma pieced before she died."

"No," said Wangero. "I don't want those. They are stitched around the borders by machine."

"That'll make them last better," I said.

"That's not the point," said Wangero. "These are all pieces of dresses Grandma used to wear. She did all this stitching by hand. Imagine!" She held the quilts securely in her arms, stroking them.

"Some of the pieces, like those lavender ones, come from old clothes her mother handed down to her," I said, moving up to touch the quilts. Dee (Wangero) moved back just enough so that I couldn't reach the quilts. They already belonged to her.

"Imagine!" she breathed again, clutching them closely to her bosom.

"The truth is," I said, "I promised to give them quilts to Maggie, for when she marries John Thomas."

She gasped like a bee had stung her.

"Maggie can't appreciate these quilts!" she said. "She'd probably be backward enough to put them to everyday use."

"I reckon she would," I said. "God knows I been saving 'em for long enough with nobody using 'em. I hope she will!" I didn't want to bring up how I had offered Dee (Wangero) a quilt when she went away to college. Then she had told me they were old-fashioned, out of style.

"But they're *priceless*!" she was saying now, furiously; for she has a temper. "Maggie would put them on the bed and in five years they'd be in rags. Less than that!"

"She can always make some more," I said. "Maggie knows how to quilt."

Dee (Wangero) looked at me with hatred. "You just will not understand. The point is these quilts, *these* quilts!"

"Well," I said stumped. "What would *you* do with them?"

"Hang them," she said. As if that was the only thing you *could* do with quilts.

Maggie by now was standing in the door. I could almost hear the sound her feet made as they scraped over each other.

"She can have them, Mama," she said, like somebody used to never winning anything, or having anything reserved for her. "I can 'member Grandma Dee without the quilts."

I looked at her hard. She had filled her bottom lip with checkerberry snuff and it gave her face a kind of dopey, hangdog look. It was Grandma Dee and Big Dee who taught her how to quilt herself. She stood there with her scarred hands hidden in the folds of her skirt. She looked at her sister with something like fear but she wasn't mad at her. This was Maggie's portion. This was the way she knew God to work.

When I looked at her like that something hit me in the top of my head and ran down to the soles of my feet. Just like when I'm in church and the spirit of God touches me and I get happy and shout. I did something I never had done before: hugged Maggie to me, then dragged her on into the room, snatched the quilts out of Miss Wangero's hands and dumped them into Maggie's lap. Maggie just sat there on my bed with her mouth open.

"Take one or two of the others," I said to Dee.

But she turned without a word and went out to Hakim-a-barber.

"You just don't understand," she said, as Maggie and I came out to the car.

"What don't I understand?" I wanted to know.

"Your heritage," she said. And then she turned to Maggie, kissed her, and said, "You ought to try to make something of yourself, too, Maggie. It's really a new day for us. But from the way you and Mama still live you'd never know it."

She put on some sunglasses that hid everything above the tip of her nose and her chin.

Maggie smiled; maybe at the sunglasses. But a real smile, not scared. After we watched the car dust settle I asked Maggie to bring me a dip of snuff. And then the two of us sat there just enjoying, until it was time to go in the house and go to bed.

Lydia Y. Minatoya

from
Talking to High Monks in the Snow

In her autobiography, Lydia Minatoya describes her experiences as a Japanese American both in the United States and in Asia. In these selections, she details her early childhood.

Transformation

PERHAPS IT BEGINS WITH MY NAMING. During her pregnancy, my mother was reading Dr. Spock. "Children need to belong," he cautioned. "An unusual name can make them the subject of ridicule." My father frowned when he heard this. He stole a worried glance at my sister. Burdened by her Japanese name, Misa played unsuspectingly on the kitchen floor.

The Japanese know full well the dangers of conspicuousness. "The nail that sticks out gets pounded down," cautions an old maxim. In America, Relocation was all the proof they needed.

And so it was, with great earnestness, my parents searched for a conventional name. They wanted me to have the full true promise of America.

"I will ask my colleague Froilan," said my father. "He is the smartest man I know."

"And he has poetic soul," said my mother, who cared about such things.

In due course, Father consulted Froilan. He gave Froilan his conditions for suitability.

"First, if possible, the full name should be alliterative," said my father. "Like Misa Minatoya." He closed his eyes and sang my sister's name. "Second, if not an alliteration, at least the name should have assonantal rhyme."

"Like Misa Minatoya?" said Froilan with a teasing grin.

"Exactly," my father intoned. He gave an emphatic nod. "Finally, most importantly, the name must be readily recognizable as conventional." He peered at Froilan with hope. "Do you have any suggestions or ideas?"

Froilan, whose own American child was named Ricardito, thought a while.

"We already have selected the name for a boy," offered my Father. "Eugene."

"Eugene?" wondered Froilan. "But it meets none of your conditions!"

"Eugene is a special case," said my father, "after Eugene, Oregon, and Eugene O'Neill. The beauty of the Pacific Northwest, the power of a great writer."

"I see," said Froilan, who did not but who realized that this naming business would be more complex than he had anticipated. "How about Maria?"

"Too common," said my father. "We want a *conventional* name, not a common one."

"Hmmm," said Froilan, wondering what the distinction was. He thought some more and then brightened. "Lydia!" he declared. He rhymed the name with media. "Lydia for *la bonita infanta!*"

And so I received my uncommon conventional name. It really did not provide the camouflage my parents had anticipated. I remained unalterably alien. For Dr. Spock had been addressing *American* families, and in those days, everyone knew all real American families were white.

Call it denial, but many Japanese Americans never quite understood that the promise of America was not truly meant for them. They lived in horse stalls at the Santa Anita racetrack and said the Pledge of Allegiance daily. They rode to Relocation Camps under armed guard, labeled with numbered tags, and sang "The Star-Spangled Banner." They lived in deserts or swamps, ludicrously imprisoned—where would they run if they ever escaped—and formed garden clubs, and yearbook staffs, and citizen town meetings. They even elected beauty queens.

My mother practiced her okoto and was featured in a recital. She taught classes in fashion design and her students mounted a show. Into exile she had carried an okoto and a sewing machine. They were her past and her future. She believed in Art and Technology.

My mother's camp was the third most populous city in the entire state of Wyoming. Across the barren lands, behind barbed wire, bloomed these little oases of democracy. The older generation bore the humiliation with pride. "*Kodomo no tame ni,*" they said. For the sake of the children. They thought that if their dignity was great, then their children would be spared. Call it valor. Call it bathos. Perhaps it was closer to slapstick: a sweet and bitter lunacy.

Call it adaptive behavior. Coming from a land swept by savage typhoons, ravaged by earthquakes and volcanoes, the Japanese have evolved a view of the world: a cooperative, stoic, almost magical way of thinking. Get along, work hard, and never quite see the things that can bring you pain. Against the tyranny of nature, of feudal lords, of wartime hysteria, the charm works equally well.

And so my parents gave me an American name and hoped that I could pass. They nourished me with the American dream: Opportunity, Will, Transformation.

When I was four and my sister was eight, Misa regularly used me as a comic foil. She would bring her playmates home from school and query me as I sat amidst the milk bottles on the front steps.

"What do you want to be when you grow up?" she would say. She would nudge her audience into attentiveness.

"A mother kitty cat!" I would enthuse. Our cat had just delivered her first litter of kittens and I was enchanted by the rasping tongue and soft mewings of motherhood.

"And what makes you think you can become a cat?" Misa would prompt, gesturing to her howling friends—wait for this; it gets better yet.

"This is America," I stoutly would declare. "I can grow up to be anything that I want!"

My faith was unshakable. I believed. Opportunity. Will. Transformation.

Albany, 1958

THE METER OF MY CHILDHOOD was the rising and plunging of a sewing machine needle: rapid and smooth, like an endless distant drum roll. My mother hummed as she sewed. She guided the fabric this way and that.

In 1938, my mother had graduated from a school of costume design. Before she was sent to a Relocation Camp, she had her own boutique in Beverly Hills. It was her dream come true. At that time, her brother was working as a houseboy in a Beverly Hills mansion. One heat-shimmering day, the movie star Ginger Rogers had smiled at him. She had stopped him as he trudged to the bus stop and had given him a ride in her shiny new sports car. Down the sloping boulevard and toward the city of angels. It was before the war, a time and place when anything could happen, when the dream of America had never seemed finer.

The Albany of my childhood was a festive place, closer in spirit to the nineteenth century than to the twenty-first. Italian pushcart grocers crowded southern city blocks, crafting tiered architectural wonders from fresh produce and pungent sausages. The clamor of market day hung in the air mingling with garlic and yeast.

In that Albany, heavy-legged workhorses clopped along cobblestones, delivering bread from German bakeries and milk from Dutch dairies. A cable car ran along streets named for trees that once had grown there—chestnut, elm—or for birds that no longer were seen. We had an icebox instead of a refrigerator, and a short solid man who sang opera as he delivered the ice. My mother washed laundry against a wooden scrub board in a claw-footed bathtub. My sister hung it in the yard.

Each year in early April, an annual dinner-dance was sponsored by the pharmaceutical institute where my father worked as a researcher. A ballroom was rented in a downtown hotel. Musicians were hired to play big-band music. The dinner-dance was the only time when my mother would sew for herself. It was the one time when my parents went out, alone, together. I was a romantic child, dreamy and diffuse. For me, the dinner-dance was an annual event: looked forward to in long anticipation and back upon with nostalgia.

Each year, on a snowy weekday evening, Father would take us window shopping. The deserted downtown streets would be a magical glaze of snow-softened Christmas lights and shadowy shop displays. We would walk quietly, measuredly, as if in a museum. My mother would linger in front of the mannequins clad in evening apparel. My sister would glitter with questions. "How do they get that Santa's hand to wave? When will we get our tree?" I would follow along, drunk with wonder: tilting my face to the soft swirling sky, trying to taste snowflakes with the tip of my tongue.

Each year before the tape had desiccated on the backs of the New Year's cards and they had fallen, first into dizzying angles, and then to the floor, my mother would have decided on the design for her dinner-dance dress. Then there would be a trip to the fabric store. I would run my hands along graduated rainbows of thread spools. I would listen to their wobbling sound and watch their changing hues as they shimmered in the light.

As the dress took form, my parents would practice dancing.

"Slow, slow, quick, quick, slow," Father would mutter with determination as he trod unmincingly on Okaa-chan's feet and guided her into the walls.

"Next lady?" he gallantly would inquire. Misa and I would take turns, balancing on the tops of his shoes, as Father swept us around the room.

I always thought that Dinner-Dance Eve had some of the magic of Christmas. Every year, I would perch on the bathtub's edge. I would watch my father fix his tie. "See the nice dimple below the knot?" Father would turn from the mirror and bend to show me. "The dimple is very important." I solemnly would nod—the honored recipient of this arcane cultural wisdom.

Back in the bedroom, Okaa-chan would slide into her new dress. She would glance at her reflection with modest pleasure. When she moved, I could catch the light sweet scent of face powder.

When I was seven or eight, the window shopping and the dinner-dances stopped. The granite façades of the downtown stores were grimy with graffiti. Display windows were boarded with plywood. The elegant hotels had fallen into disrepair. No one danced to big-band music anymore.

As I grew older, my mother began to sew for wealthy women. The women lived in country homes where sunlight, reflected from swimming pools just beyond French doors, played across fine wood floors.

Once after a luncheon in the city, a woman came to our house for a fitting. Standing erect in the doorway, then bowing slightly, my mother met her formally.

"Won't you please come in? May I please take your coat?"

"Here you go. Try to put it somewhere clean."

Like an eagle, her words slipped regally down a great distance and struck with awful ease.

After the fitting, my father was ashamed and angry.

"Actually, I do not like this work," he stormed. "You do not have to do this; we do not need this kind of money." He waved his arms dismissively at Okaa-chan's sewing machine. "They come and look at our home with contempt. You kneel at their hems like a servant! *Mo dame desu yo!* It is no good, I tell you!"

Okaa-chan was intractable. Eloquent in anger, she blazed over the pronunciation of words that ordinarily would have left pondering pauses in her speech. "I do not care what they think of me, of our home. They cannot affect our value." My mother stepped in front of her sewing machine, as if to shield it from scorn. "My work gives me happiness." She squarely faced my father. "I do not care if you speak as Husband," she said daringly. "I am a Designer!"

"You are a seamstress," snorted my father.

The New House

WE LIVED ON A STREET that mirrored the social climate of the times. Two blocks north was the Park District. There, behind the broad bay windows of brownstones, existed the slightly shabby offices of struggling doctors and dentists. Within attics and basements dwelled students of law and medicine. On the southeast corner of the Park District, Mr. Rheingold owned a drugstore. He was a kindly man, most often found dispensing candy to the neighborhood children and academic exhortations to his growing sons.

South of the Park District, buildings turned to brick. Here lived the meat packers and deliverymen: the Polish and Irish families. At midblock, the houses suddenly dropped from four to three stories and narrowed from three to two windows. This juncture, of sudden diminishment, was where my family lived. To our north stood a larger house, once more grand. It was occupied by white families who had fallen upon misfortune: a widow who in 1898 had come as a bride, an elevator operator who in a work-related incident had lost his right hand, his polio-stricken wife.

To our south, where the houses shifted from brick to wood, lived the black families and a couple who was blind. To me, the blind couple seemed misplaced. White and white-collared, they should have lived to our north. But their pale, staring eyes left the neighborhood uneasy and, in any event, they cared little about their ranking in an ordering of melanin.

When Misa and I were children, we had a method for calculating the ages of our friends' mothers. "If Darlene is six years old, then her mother must be twenty-one," Misa would estimate. She could do the arithmetic in her head.

The formula Misa used involved adding fifteen years to the age of any given playmate. In our neighborhood, girls grew to adolescence, became pregnant, and left school. One, two, three.

When Misa turned ten, my parents began to talk together late at night. They wanted to move to a suburban neighborhood. They wanted to live in a district where daughters were expected to graduate from four-year colleges or universities. "Someday," Okaa-chan would say to Misa, as a lure, "someday you will receive matching set of Samsonite luggage. You will pack it with plaid, pleated skirts, and you will go away to college." Okaa-chan would hesitate; her knowledge of the coed experience would falter. Misa would shrug with indifference and continue to draw cartoons of pretty mice wearing pretty clothes. The opportunity to learn was more Okaa-chan's dream than hers.

Alarmed, Okaa-chan refocused her attention on the drafting of blueprints. She designed a simple house: three bedrooms, an attached garage, and a room with Japanese shoji screens. Father began to look for a lot. He based his search on the percentages of National Merit Scholars within a school district's graduating class. Evening after evening, he would wash our powder blue Chevrolet. We would put on our nice clothes. Then we would go to look at lots. When we arrived, the lots were never available. Someone had just purchased them; the prices had been raised. It was puzzling to me.

"Never mind," Father would say as he drove us home, "soon we will build our house."

"See the gardens Misa, Yuri-chan?" Okaa-chan would say. "Someday you will have one too."

"And a bicycle, and a dog?" I eagerly would ask.

"Moron," Misa angrily would hiss. "Don't you know when to shut up?"

"Takes one to know one," I happily would chant. At the age of six, I was the only one who loved those evening drives.

In a small town, on the eastern side of the Hudson River, my parents bought a lot. It was lushly wooded. Each weekend my father prepared a picnic lunch—Japanese rice balls and a can of sardines—and went to clear the trees. The lunches made him nostalgic.

"Your grandfather supervised a stretch of line along the Great Northern Railroad," he explained as he formed the rice balls. "During the Depression, the boxcars would roll by our house in the desert. They would make a lonesome sound." Father salted the rice balls to the rhythm of a rocking train. "Ka chun, ka chun, ka chun."

He paused a moment in recollection. "Hobos would be silhouetted along the tops of the cars like crows along a telephone line."

"Where were they going?"

"They crisscrossed the country endlessly. No work to do; no place to go. Your grandfather would feel sorry for them. He would leave cans of sardines and balls of rice down by the railroad tracks. The hobos would jump from the rolling cars and squat to eat the food. They would walk, wavering through a prism of desert heat, like zombies coming from another dimension. They would come toward our house, getting bigger as they came."

"Weren't you scared?"

"Up close, they lost their strangeness. I could see they were just tired men. They came to help with the chores and to tell their sad hobo tales."

One October dusk, when the new house was almost complete, our family went to see the lot. Misa and Okaa-chan explored the house. Father and I stood in the front yard.

"In the spring, myrtle will grow around the base of the dogwood tree over there," he said to me. "The tree will billow with blossoms."

I looked past the dogwood tree. Six or seven adults were approaching. I felt a chill.

Father glanced at the walkers. "The myrtle will be deep green," he continued, "with a sprinkling of small purple flowers."

The adults had reached the edge of our property. They stood there quite close, and jostled restlessly.

"When the dogwood has finished blooming, red berries will form," said my father. I slipped my hand in his.

"Hey, you!"

"Good evening," Father turned his attention from me: slowly, deliberately, dangerously. "Is it I whom you wish to address?"

"We live in this neighborhood and it has always been a nice neighborhood."

The others rumbled in assent.

"We are clean, decent people and we don't intend to see our neighborhood's ruin!"

"I am sincerely glad to hear that," said my father. He spoke with careful calm. "We, too, are clean, decent people. We expect our neighbors to act in decent ways."

"We just came to welcome you," said the spokesman, suddenly shifting his style. "You might say we're a hospitality committee, here to help you understand our ways."

Once when I was five years old, a strange woman had given me a penny, had walked up to me in a department store when my mother was occupied with a purchase, had seized me by the hand and pressed hard. "And what do you say?" she had wheezed excitedly, her pallid face flushed in splotches and forced close to mine. "And what do you say?" The scene flooded back as I stood by my father's side. The pain of the penny biting into my palm, the horror of her excited face, the self-disgust when, once again, I heard myself whisper, "Thank you."

When we moved to the new house, I was nervous about my first day of school. I wanted to belong. My father misread my anxiety. "A bus will take you from the corner of the street to school," he carefully explained. "After school, a bus will bring you home."

On the first morning, I boarded the yellow bus. "How much is the fare, sir?" I asked.

"Don't talk to the driver, stay behind the white line," he growled.

I did not move. I was a city child. I knew there was no such thing as a free bus ride. "Do I pay at the end? Do I buy a book of coupons? Are there tokens?" I persisted.

The children on the bus began to giggle.

The school bus took us past pasturelands. Cows grazed in morning meadows. Outside of picture books, I had never even seen a cow. They were as exotic as elephants. "There are *cows* out there!" I screamed, pointing.

The children glanced at the cows with disinterest. Their interest had fastened on me.

In school, during recess, my classmates gathered around me.

"What religion are you?" asked a fair-haired, freckled boy. His hair smelled faintly of tonic, just like a grown-up man.

The other children stiffened. I knew that this was the test.

"Uhmmm . . . I'm Christian," I nervously said.

"Silly. *Everyone* is Christian!"

I was surprised. This had not been true in Albany.

"Well?"

"I guess I'm Protestant."

A girl with long auburn barrel curls tossed her head with impatience. "Everyone is Protestant!" she declared. Her voice dropped to a conspiratorial whisper. "Except Licia. She's Catholic." The children shot a quick glance at a shy, slender girl sitting alone by the window. That's Licia, I thought. As if disturbed by my identifying gaze, Licia shifted uneasily in her seat.

"So . . . what religion *are* you?" the freckled boy was growing testy.

"Methodist!" I blurted with the relief of sudden recollection.

The children relaxed. "Me too," smiled one. "I'm a Methodist too!"

I grinned. I knew that I had passed.

My classmates went home and told their parents that there was a new Methodist girl in school. The next few days went well. It must have been the teachers who spread the news that I was more than Methodist. By the end of the week, my classmates had learned of a new category: more taboo than being Catholic, more indicative of bad blood than being adopted. My classmates had learned about color.